You don't have to be Jewish to enjoy the uproarious jokes presented in this treasury of Jewish humor.

Full of both pathos and belly laughs, this book exuberantly taps the rich tradition and delightful variety of Jewish humor. They're all here—the amusing and instructive stories told by Rabbis in the ''Old Country;'' the warm, funny tales about Jewish immigrants; and hilarious jokes told by stand-up comics in the Borscht Belt.

As nourishing as chicken soup and Jewish mothers, this bittersweet humor tells of Jews in the flush of success; tells about the brilliant and the bumbling, the big shots and the beggars, the devout and the impious.

Here's a book to make you laugh with tears in your eyes.

Enjoy! Enjoy!

SIMON R. POLLACK

Jewish Wit
FOR ALL OCCASIONS

A HART BOOK

A & W VISUAL LIBRARY • NEW YORK

PUBLISHED BY
A & W PUBLSHERS, INC.
95 MADISON AVENUE
NEW YORK, NEW YORK 10016

LIBRARY OF CONGRESS CATALOG CARD NO. 79-65341

ISBN: 0-89104-153-2

Printed in Canada

Jewish Wit

FOR ALL OCCASIONS

Speak Up!

Sammy wanted to buy his mother a gift for her birthday, but not just the same old thing; he wanted something different.

So he went into a pet shop and asked the man for suggestions. Well, it just so happened that they had a parrot who could speak seven languages. Sammy considered that as unique a gift as one could buy, so he had the bird sent to his mother.

The following week, Sammy called to find out how his mother liked the gift. "It was wonderful," she said. "At first, it seemed that such a small bird might be a little tough, but the soup was delicious."

Sammy hollered into the phone, "Ma! You *ate* the bird! Why, that parrot could speak seven languages!"

Whereupon she retorted, "If that's so, why when he saw me taking out the pot, didn't he say something?"

POOR MRS. EISENBERG was beside herself. Her husband had left her, and her daughter Sally was thirty-two years old and still unmarried. She thought about it and worried about it and finally decided to take some action.

"Sally," she said, "I think you ought to put an advertisement in the paper." Sally was aghast at the thought.

"No, listen," said Mrs. Eisenberg, "it sounds wild, but I think we should try it. You don't put your name in, just a box number. Here, I wrote one up already." And she showed Sally an ad she had devised:

> *Charming Jewish Girl, Well-Educated, Fine Cook, Would like to Meet Kind, Intelligent, Educated, Jewish Gentleman. Object: Matrimony.*

Sally was embarrassed, but she couldn't talk her mother out of it. So into the paper the ad went. And Sally went every day to see if there were any replies.

A few days later, there was a letter for her. Sally ran home to her mother flushed with excitement. "Look!" she cried.

"Well, hurry up and open it!" urged Mrs. Eisenberg. So Sally tore open the envelope and unfolded the letter. Then she began to cry.

"What's the matter?" asked Mrs. Eisenberg.

Sally's sobs got even louder. "It's from Papa!"

Logic Triumphs

Ethel lay in bed freezing; the draft from the open window ran icy cold through her blanket. But her husband Sam was snoring deeply, unaware of his spouse's discomfort.

Finally Ethel could take it no longer. She propped herself up on an elbow and poked a finger in her husband's stomach. "Sam, Sam, it's cold outside," she exhorted. "Sam, close the window." But Sam didn't move.

Ethel tried again. "Sam, *Sam!*" She shook her husband's shoulder. "Get up and close the window. It's cold outside!"

Now Sam awoke, somewhat furious. "So if I close the window," he growled, "will it be warm outside?"

SADIE WASN'T FEELING WELL, and she knew she should see a doctor. So she asked her friend Becky the name of the doctor she used.

"His name's Feinstein," said Becky, "but you should know he's expensive."

"How expensive?" asked Sadie.

"Well, it's fifty dollars for the first visit, and twenty-five for every visit after that."

So Sadie went off to see Dr. Feinstein. When her turn came to be examined, she smiled brightly and said to the nurse, "Hi, honey. Here I am again!"

A MIDDLE-AGED WOMAN accompanied her husband on a business trip to London. During the day, he was busy with his appointments, so the lady set off for some shopping.

At the end of her spree, she found herself near Fortnum and Mason's, and remembered their internationally renowned confections. So she went in and selected several tins of biscuits and candies, as well as some jars of marmalade, to keep at the hotel.

"Where shall we deliver these, madam?" asked the salesman.

"Oh, that's all right," responded the American lady, "I'll take them."

The salesman thought she didn't understand. "The delivery is free, madam. We'll be glad to send it."

"I know," the lady replied, "but I really don't mind."

"That's very nice of you, madam, but still, why *shlep*?"

The Jewish Cow

Sol had a dairy farm in the country where he bred beautiful golden Guernsey cows and also the lovely black-and-white Holsteins.

One day Jake, a friend from the city, came to visit and suggested, "Sol, why don't you cross-breed your cows. There's a fortune to be made in cross-breeding."

Sol thought it sounded like a good idea. "What have I got to lose," he mused. So he tried it. Sometime later, the friend came back to visit. "How did the experiment go?" he asked Sol.

"Well," answered Sol, "I did like you said. I cross-bred the golden Guernsey with the Holstein. And what I got I called a Goldstein. But nobody wanted to buy it!"

"Why was that?" queried Jake.

"Why? Because," answered Sol, "when a customer looked over all the other cows, each of them said, 'Moo-oo!' But when the man came over to my Goldstein, she eyed him and said 'Nuu-uu.'"

THE STAR SALESMAN was doing great. Rubin and Cohen were shipping dresses at an enormous rate. It's true that Sid Metofsky drew $600 a week, but he was certainly piling up the orders.

Only one thing bothered the partners. On top of his draw, and on top of a heavy expense account for travel, every so often Metofsky sent in an extra item of $50 with a notation, "A man isn't made of wood."

When this expense item appeared for the third time, Cohen looked at Rubin and he said, "What should we do about this?"

"Well, considering the business he's sending in, we just better overlook it and pay up," answered Rubin.

But the following week, three tabs came in for fifty smackers each, and each tab read, "A man isn't made of wood."

Rubin counseled forbearing, but Cohen lost his temper. "Three times in two days!" he bellowed. "Miss Jacobs!" he called to his secretary. "Send a telegram to Metofsky. 'Dear Sid: Wood, no. But a man isn't made of iron either.'"

Would You Mind Repeating That?

Mr. Levy went to see his lawyer. He was quite distraught. "What am I going to do?" he asked. "Finkel is suing me for breaking an irreplaceable jar of his!"

The lawyer seemed calm. "Don't worry, Mr. Levy," he soothed. "We have at least three lines of defense. In the first place, we will prove that you never borrowed the jar from Finkel. In the second place, we'll prove that when you borrowed the jar, it was already damaged beyond repair. And in the third place, we'll prove that when you returned it, it was in absolutely perfect condition."

MINNIE HAD BEEN DEPRESSED, so she decided to try going to a psychiatrist. Perhaps he would do her some good. She made an appointment with Dr. Oglethorpe, recommended by her family doctor.

After one session with Minnie, Dr. Oglethorpe realized the usual methods wouldn't work. So he said to her, "With your permission, I'd like to try something somewhat different. I'm going to leave the room for half an hour, and I want you to lie here on this couch and think about sex. Nothing else, just sex. When I come back, we'll talk about it."

The doctor left the room for half an hour, and when he returned, he sat down next to her with pencil and pad. "So, Minnie, tell me what you've been thinking about."

"All I could think of," said Minnie, "is that, at least for me, Saks—even though it's on Fifth Avenue—can't compare with Macy's."

IN A HOSPITAL in New York's Lower East Side, two women had each just given birth. Back in their own room again, one woman said to the other, Mazel Tov! and Mrs. Teitlebaum, what are you naming your latest?"

The second woman replied, "Qadaffi."

"Are you kidding?" the first lady cried.

"Certainly not!" affirmed the other. "I was never more serious in my life."

"Well, I guess you can name your child whatever you feel like. But, Mrs. Teitlebaum, are you sure that's the name you want?"

"Yes, I'm sure!" said the woman icily. "And by the way, I'm not Mrs. Teitlebaum, I'm *Miss* Teitlebaum."

Sense of Confidence

After years of working hard and saving, a New York couple finally had accumulated enough money to take a trip to Israel.

They toured the entire country and spent time in the big cities as well. One evening in Tel Aviv, they decided to see what the Israeli night life was like.

So they went to a night club. They enjoyed the singer tremendously. But, unfortunately for them, the comedian did his entire act in Hebrew. The wife sat patiently in silence throughout the monologue.

Her husband, however, laughed uproariously at every joke. The woman was, to say the least, surprised.

"So how come you laughed so much?" she asked when the act was over. "I didn't know you knew Hebrew."

"I don't," said the husband. "But I trusted him!"

NATALIA WAS AT HOME in Russia with her elderly aunt when suddenly the door burst open and two burly Cossacks entered.

"All right, you two. Any more at home? We intend to rape every woman in the house!" they announced.

Natalia threw herself in front of her aunt and cried, "Do whatever you will with me, but please spare my aging aunt!"

At this, the aunt pushed the young girl aside. "Why are you interfering, Natalia? A pogrom is a pogrom!"

And Don't Ask Again

Mrs. Christianson lived right near an army base. She always felt sorry for the soldiers around holidays; they were so friendless, so far away from home. So one year she decided to invite some enlisted men to join her family for Thanksgiving dinner.

She called the company sergeant and asked him to send three soldiers over for Thanksgiving dinner the following day. "Thank you, ma'am," said the sergeant.

"Oh, that's all right," said Mrs. Christianson. "But, sergeant, I almost forgot. Please, I do not wish any soldiers of the Jewish faith."

"I understand, ma'am," said the sergeant.

On Thursday, Mrs. Christianson prepared a fine, traditional turkey dinner with all the trimmings. Promptly at five o'clock, the family answered the doorbell to greet their dinner guests. Three black soldiers stood in the doorway.

Mrs. Christianson was aghast. "But," she gasped, "your sergeant must have made a mistake!"

"No, ma'am," smiled one of the soldiers. "Sergeant Greenstein never makes mistakes."

A CONSTRUCTION FIRM had just finished building an attractive apartment house in New York's upper West Side. The officers of the firm had come around to admire their work.

Just then the owner, a feisty Hebrew, came along. "By the way," asked one of the construction men, "what are you going to call the building?"

Proudly, the owner answered, "I'm calling it the Cloister Apartments."

"Great name!" remarked the construction president, "but there's no church near here, and certainly not a cloister."

"Yes," answered the owner, "but the building is cloister the subway, cloister Central Park, cloister the river, and cloister my heart!"

MAX THE TAILOR and his wife had finally saved up enough to move their family to the suburbs.

Thrilled with his new home, Max concluded that all those years of toiling had been worthwhile.

But soon Max became the object of numerous appeals from the local synagogue. They wanted him to join; they wanted him to pay dues.

"Why?" the tailor asked forthrightly. "Why should I join?"

The temple representative tried to play on Max's sense of responsibility: "So that your children will realize they're Jewish."

Whereupon Max shrugged. "Oh that! They already realize they're Jewish," he said. "They all suffer from heartburn."

Fair's Fair

Abe said to his friend Willie, "Willie, lend me twenty dollars."

Willie took out his wallet and handed Abe a ten dollar bill.

"Willie," said Abe, "I asked you for twenty."

"Yes, I know," said Willie. "This way you lose ten and I lose ten."

MR. AND MRS. GOTBAUM celebrated thirty years of marriage by going to a fancy restaurant. Awed by the elegant ambience, they nevertheless enjoyed selecting and tasting the strange-sounding dishes.

At the end of the meal, however, the waiter brought over two finger bowls and left them at the table. Mrs. Gotbaum looked at Mr. Gotbaum, and Mr. Gotbaum looked back at Mrs. Gotbaum. Neither of them knew what to do.

"Ask the waiter," suggested Mrs. Gotbaum.

"Are you kidding?" exclaimed her husband. "Show our ignorance? How embarrassing!"

"Yes," she said, "but it would be more embarrassing not to use them at all."

"True," said the man. So he called over the waiter and said, "Pardon me, but could you tell me the purpose of these dishes—of—of liquid?"

The waiter was polite. "Sir, those are finger bowls. You dip your fingers into the perfumed waters and then dry them on your napkin."

Mr. Gotbaum waited until the waiter left. Then he turned to his wife, and said, "See, Molly? You ask a foolish question, and you get a foolish answer!"

SADIE WEINTRAUB asked for two bagels.

"That'll be forty cents, please," said the baker.

"Forty cents!" exclaimed Sadie. "Why, that's twenty cents a bagel! The man across the street only charges 12 cents!"

"So, buy them across the street," shrugged the baker.

"But they're all out of bagels across the street," said Sadie.

"Lady, when I'm all out of bagels, I only charge a nickel apiece."

Staving Off the Worst

Nat was upset. "Irving, I lost my wallet and it had three hundred dollars in it!" he lamented.

Irving tried to help Nat think. "Did you look everywhere for it?" he asked. "What about your coat pockets?"

Nat said, "Sure I looked. I tried all my coat pockets, all my vest pockets, my front pants pockets, and my left hip pocket—and it just isn't anywhere."

"Your left hip pocket? Why don't you try your right hip pocket?" asked Irving.

"Well," replied Nat, "that's the last pocket I have."

"So?"

"So, if I look in that pocket and if I don't find the wallet there, I'll drop dead!"

A JEWISH MENTAL PATIENT was causing quite a stir in the institution because he wouldn't eat the food.

"I'm kosher!" shouted Moskowitz. "I won't eat this food. I want kosher meals!"

So the staff hired a Jewish woman from the community to cook special kosher meals for Moskowitz. Everybody was envious, for Moskowitz's meals were much better than theirs.

Friday night rolled around, and Moskowitz pushed back his chair after a delicious chicken dinner, and lit up a big black cigar. This was too much for the director, who called Moskowitz into his office.

"Now see here, Moskowitz. You're getting away with murder. You get the best meals because you claim you only eat kosher food. And now, on Friday night, on your Sabbath, you flout your religion, and smoke a cigar!"

Moskowitz merely shrugged his shoulders. "Why are you arguing with me?" he said. "I'm crazy, ain't I?"

COHEN WAS WALKING in the hot sun on a steaming summer day when suddenly he fainted. Passersby rushed up to him, trying to help.

"Get a doctor!" someone cried.

"Call the police!" shouted another.

"Water! Water!" hollered a third.

At that, Cohen opened one eye. Gasping, he called out, "Please, make it a seltzer!"

WHEN NASSER WAS VISITING New York City in order to attend a meeting at the United Nations, he spent one afternoon seeing the sights of the city.

It happened that the Egyptian president was down by the East River when he leaned over too far and fell in. Hearing the holler for help, a fourteen-year-old boy came running. With some strenuous tugging, he was able to pull the Egyptian out of the water.

"I owe my life to you," said Nasser. "What is your name?"

"My name is Israel Cohen, Mr. Nasser."

"Oh, you know who I am?"

"Yes, sir."

"I'm very grateful to you. I'll give you anything you want or do anything you wish."

The boy didn't think twice. "I want just one thing. Please don't tell my father!"

If I Do Say So Myself

Two men sat next to each other on the train to Miami. Since it was a long trip, both were willing to chat.

One man, obviously wealthy, opened the conversation, "I'm looking forward to being at my vacation home again. I can't wait to go golfing. I love golf. Do you play?"

The other man did not want to appear uncivilized, so he said, "Of course. I love to golf also. Why, every afternoon since my retirement I've played."

"Oh, then you must be pretty good!" said the rich man. "I play in the low seventies myself," he added modestly.

"Oh, so do I," said the second man. "Of course, if it gets any colder, I go right back to the hotel!"

MRS. ROSENBUSH was negotiating for a mink stole at Mendelovitch's. She asked a lot of questions.

"If I buy the coat and I get caught in the rain," she asked the salesmen, "will it get ruined?"

"Look, lady," answered Mendelovitch, "did you ever see a mink carrying an umbrella?"

Did I Say That?

Willie loved to play golf, but the only course anywhere near his house belonged to a country club that wouldn't accept Jews. "No problem," thought Willie. "I'll just call myself William, and they'll never guess I'm Jewish." Sure enough, he was accepted.

So the very next day, Willie went onto the course, found some partners, and began to play. On the fourth hole, however, after a very careful swing, poor Willie missed the ball completely. Instinctively, he let out a holler. "*Oy gevalt!*" he shrieked.

Suddenly realizing what he had said, Willie smiled broadly and added with a flourish, "Whatever *that* means!"

AFTER MANY YEARS in the United States, Hymowitz ran into his old friend Linsky, whom he had not seen since they had been together on the boat coming over from Europe.

"How's things, Linsky?" asked Hymowitz.

"Couldn't be better," said Linsky. "I made a lot of money, have a beautiful wife, and I just celebrated the birth of my eighth child."

"That sounds great," said Hymowitz. "I guess you have a real easy life, eh?"

"Easy? It's fabulous!" replied Linsky. "I get up in the morning, have a big breakfast, then lay on my verandah. Later, maybe I'll play a round of golf, or take a walk. Then I have some lunch, and lay on my verandah again for a while. Maybe six, seven o'clock I'll have myself some supper, smoke a fine cigar, and lay once again on my verandah. And in the evening I go to the theater or maybe the ballet."

"That's just wonderful!" said the admiring Hymowitz. And the old acquaintances parted.

"That Linsky sure leads a good life," he sighed. "House, wife, eight children."

"What's his wife's name?" asked Mrs. Hymowitz.

"Such a fancy name she's got," replied her husband. "He calls her 'Verandah.'"

ONE HOT SUMMER DAY, Mr. and Mrs. Blumberg took their little boy on a rare outing to the beach.

Mr. Blumberg promptly stretched out under a beach umbrella and went to sleep, while Mrs. Blumberg and David carried on their usual round of verbal and physical activity.

"David, David, come here. Don't run into the water. You'll get drowned!

"David, don't play with the sand. You'll get it in your eyes.

"David, David, don't stand in the sun. You'll get sunstroke.

"Oy, vey!" she wailed, "Such a nervous child."

A Slip of the Lip

Goldberg, the feisty neighborhood tailor, at the age of sixty-six decided he was tired of working and retired. Within a week, restlessness set in.

One afternoon, Goldberg left the house for a walk. He strolled along and soon found himself in a section of the city he'd never been in before. Soon, he came upon a convent, where two nuns sat in a grassy courtyard.

He hailed the nuns, and they greeted him kindly. Goldberg asked if they had any need for a tailor in the establishment. "I'll work cheap," he said. "Money I don't need. I need a little part-time job, it should occupy my time."

So Goldberg began to work at the convent. He was happy, his wife was happy, and the nuns were happy, too. One day, however, a Sister came to him with a message.

"Mr. Goldberg, you're a fine craftsman, and we're very content with your work," she said. "But I have a favor to ask of you. When you speak to the Mother Superior, please don't call her 'Mother Shapiro.'"

EIGHTY-YEAR-OLD HESCHEL had been sitting on his front porch when he saw two cars crash on the street in front of him. So when the case came to court, Heschel was called as a witness.

Seated in the witness box, he listened carefully to the prosecutor's questions. "How old are you?" he was asked.

Heschel answered, "I'm eighty years old till a hundred and twenty."

"Just answer the question, please. How old are you?"

"I'm eighty years old till a hundred and twenty, I told you."

The judge became irritated. "The witness will please answer the question and only the question! Now—"

The defense attorney rose from his seat. "Your Honor," he interjected, "may I ask the witness the same question?"

"If you wish," said the judge.

The defense attorney turned to Heschel. "Till a hundred and twenty years old, God willing, how old are you, Mr. Heschel," he asked.

"Eighty," responded Heschel.

MOLLY AND YETTA were in the middle of their once-a-month telephone call for keeping up-to-date on each other's gossip.

"Oh, and Molly," said Yetta, "did I tell you about my son David?"

"No, what about David?" asked Molly.

"He is going to a psychiatrist!" said the mother proudly. "Twice a week he goes to a psychiatrist!"

Molly knew she was supposed to be impressed, but she didn't really understand why. "Is that good?" she asked.

"Of course it's good!" exclaimed Yetta. "Fifty dollars an hour he pays, fifty dollars! And all he talks about is me!"

IN SHUL ON YOM KIPPUR, the solemn Day of Judgment, a rich Jew stood at his seat and prayed in a loud whisper, "Oh Lord, I am the lowest of the low. I am unworthy of your goodness. I am a nobody, a nothing!"

Immediately, in the row directly in back of him, a poor piece goods cutter raised his voice in prayer, "Oh Lord, my God, please forgive my sins for I am nothing!"

Whereupon, the first man turned around in disdain. "Look who claims he's a nothing!"

A HORSE PLAYER was recounting his doleful experiences at the track. "I had a very strange dream the other night. I kept dreaming about hats—all kinds of hats—men's hats, women's hats, witches' hats, big hats, little hats, hats, hats, hats. I decided the dream must be telling me something. So the next day I went to Bowie to try out my hunch. I bet on every horse that had a name that had something to do with hats. In the first race, I put 50 bucks on Fedora, and she came in first. The second race, I put 100 bucks on Straw Hat, and she beat the field by three lengths. Seeing I was on a winning streak, I put 500 bucks on a nag called Blue Bonnet in the third race, and sure enough, she won by a nose. In the fourth race, I couldn't find any horse with a hat name but I felt like a winner so I put all my winnings plus another $250 on a horse called Foul Play, and she dragged in seventh in a field of eight."

"Too bad," said his friend. "By the way, who won that race?"

"Oh," he said, "some dodo with the crazy name of Yarmulka."

Add It to the Pile

One evening, Mrs. Goldblatt sat concentrating over the family checkbook, while her husband read the newspaper. "By the way, honey," her husband mused, "what do you think we should do about the oil-depletion bill?"

Mrs. Goldblatt sighed. "Hand it over," she said, "and I'll make out a check."

THE NURSE at the front desk answered the telephone. "Hello. Can I help you?"

"Oh, nurse," came the voice, "can you please tell me how Sol Weinstein is doing?"

The nurse was kind. "Of course," she said, "just one moment while I get out his chart. . . . Well, it seems he's doing just fine! The doctor has written here that he can be released on Friday!"

"Oh, that's wonderful!" said the voice.

"And who can I tell him called?" asked the nurse.

"It's *me*! Weinstein!" said the voice. "I decided to phone you because the doctor won't tell me anything!"

Hey, Wait a Minute!

Sammy finally managed to get the new receptionist to agree to a date. The next morning, he looked pleased as punch. He told his friend Bernie all about it.

"You know that beautiful new receptionist? Well, I went out with her last night, and let me tell you, she's a living doll," Sammy bragged.

"What did you do?" asked Bernie.

"Well, I took her to dinner and a show, and then we went up to her apartment, and we got intimate. And I must say, she's a million times better than my wife, Molly."

"Gee, she sounds wonderful!" said Bernie.

"Do you mind if I ask her out?"

"No, of course not," said Sammy. "Have yourself a ball!"

So two nights later Bernie took her out. The next morning, Sammy went to Bernie's office to get a report.

"Ah, Sammy," Bernie began. "She was a lot of fun, but how can you compare her to your wife, Molly?"

HITLER WAS HAVING bad dreams, so he ordered his henchmen to find him someone to interpret them for him.

"Ah," intoned the seer, "I see that you are destined to die on a Jewish holiday."

Hitler frowned, but he was curious. "Which one?" he asked.

"It doesn't matter. Any day you die will be a Jewish holiday!"

MAX HAD LIVED A LONG and fruitful life, and he had tried to make it a virtuous one. But when he entered heaven, the angel in charge frowned at him.

"You can't stay here," said the angel. "Sorry."

"But why?" asked Max, "I always tried to be a good man."

"That's just the problem," explained the angel. "Everyone here in heaven was a good man, true, but every one of them committed at least *one* sin. It's only human. And since you didn't sin at all, the rest of the souls will resent you. I can't allow bad feelings in heaven."

"But I want to stay!" protested Max. "Isn't there something I can do?"

"Well," considered the angel, "I could let you have six more hours on earth, to see if you could find some sin to commit. But remember, it's got to be a real sin—doing some other person a real injury."

"Oh, yes," cried Max. "Please let me try. I'll find something!"

So Max went back to earth and searched around. Suddenly, he saw an opportunity. A middle-aged woman was looking at him, all smiles. Apparently she found him attractive. He engaged her in conversation and it became clear that she had the same sin in mind as he did. So he willingly went home with her.

Max spent the next few hours making the

most of his sin, till he heard the call from above that his time was up.

"Well, this was wonderful," said Max. "I'm sorry but I have to go now."

The woman smiled at him warmly and exclaimed joyously, "Oh Max! You know, in my whole life I was never married or anything. And you just gave me the best time I ever had in my entire life! What a good deed you've performed today!"

Hedging His Bets

Abe hadn't taken his wife out in a long time. So he called her into the living room and said, "Molly, I've decided something," and he slapped his hand on the couch arm for emphasis. "We're stepping out this coming Monday—if, God willing, we're alive. And if not—we'll go Tuesday."

THE PEASANT went to see his rabbi.

"Oh, rabbi! There's been a long drought, my crops have failed, my livestock are dying, and now my family is getting sick because they don't have enough to eat. What should I do?"

"Don't worry," reassured the rabbi. "God will provide."

"Oh, I know, I know," sighed the peasant. "I just wish He would provide *until* He provides."

Who Am I Speaking to, Please?

A young boy had been given some Israel Bonds for his bar mitzvah. Now he was a grown man about to be married, and he wanted to cash them in. So he went to the Bonds office in New York.

"I'd like to talk to someone about some bonds I have," the young man told the secretary at the information desk.

"Are you interested in conversion or redemption?" he was asked.

At that, the young man stepped back to look at the sign over the door. "Say," he asked, "is this Israel Bonds, or is it the Baptist Mission?"

So Correct!

Shapiro had had a very good year, so he decided to take a cruise to France for the first time in his life. He was determined to savor every part of the trip.

The first night, Shapiro was shown to his place for dinner and found himself sharing a table with a well-dressed Frenchman. When Shapiro arrived, the Frenchman rose, bowed, and declared, *"Bon appétit!"*

Shapiro replied, "Shapiro!"

This same ritual took place at every meal. On the last day of the trip, Shapiro happened to run into the purser, and took advantage of the encounter to tell him what a pleasant table companion Mr. Bon Appetit had been.

"Oh, Mr. Shapiro," said the purser, *"Bon appétit* is not his name; that's just French for 'I wish you a hearty appetite.'"

"Is that so?" said Shapiro. He couldn't wait to rectify the situation. That evening, at dinner before his companion could do a thing, Shapiro stood up, bowed ceremoniously, and declared, *"Bon appétit!"*

Whereupon the Frenchman rose and replied, "Shapiro!"

MR. PLOTNICK was reading the obituary page in the newspaper. Suddenly he turned to his wife and said to her, "Sweetheart, I hope you live to be a hundred and twenty, plus three months."

"What's this 'plus three months?'" asked his wife.

"Well," replied Plotnick, "I wouldn't want you—God forbid—to die suddenly."

A Father's Woes

A much-loved rabbi died a peaceful death, and his soul rose swiftly to heaven.

There, the rabbi was warmly greeted by hosts of angels. They wanted to honor him by dressing him in finery and escorting him through the golden streets, for he had been such a fine man. But the rabbi, inexplicably, wouldn't participate. He covered his face with his hands, and fled from the midst of the celebrations.

Astonished, the angels brought the rabbi before God himself. "My child," said the Lord, "it is on record that you have lived entirely in accord with My wishes, and yet you refuse the honors that have, most fittingly, been prepared for you. Why?"

"Oh, Most Holy One," replied the rabbi, prostrating himself, "I am not as deserving as You think. Somewhere along the way I must have sinned, for my son, heedless of my example and of my precepts, turned Christian."

"Alas, I understand entirely and I forgive," said God. "I had the same trouble myself."

BILLY GOLD WAS HAVING a little trouble with his Hebrew lessons, so his father decided to ask the rabbi if he could give him some personal attention.

After several months of private tutoring, Billy was doing a little better, but the only

Hebrew he had mastered were the first few words of the Kaddish, the prayer said for the soul of a departed parent.

Approaching the rabbi anxiously, Mr. Gold said, "I wanted you to teach him some Hebrew, that's true, but why right away the prayer for the dead? Do I look so old to you? Do you think I'm going to die any minute?"

The rabbi explained calmly, "Mr. Gold, you should only live as long as it will take your son to learn the Kaddish."

Two Irishmen and a Jew were discussing what they would do if their doctor told them they had only six months to live.

O'Rourke said, "I know what I would do. I would sell everything and move to France. And for the next six months, I'd play with all the beautiful girls Paris and the Riviera had to offer!"

McLaughlin said, "If my doctor told me I had only six months, I too would sell everything. But I think I would like to travel. I would go all around the world from East to West, and then I'd go around again from North to South."

Then it was Levy's turn. "If my doctor said I had only six months to live," he said thoughtfully, "the first thing I would do would be to get another doctor!"

YONKEL AND FLORRIE were invited to a dinner party at Yonkel's boss's home on Long Island. Yonkel knew he had to go, but he was afraid the people there would be much smarter than he. So he instructed Florrie to keep her mouth shut and not to say anything if she could help it. If someone asked her a direct question, she was to answer with just a yes or a no.

Florrie agreed, and the two set off nervously for the party. Yonkel said hardly a word the whole evening, and Florrie said nothing at all. But this state of affairs began to upset the hostess, who thought that it was her job to draw her guests into the conversation.

So the boss's wife turned to Florrie and said to her kindly, "Tell me, are you acquainted with Beethoven?"

Florrie had been silent for so long, she became flustered at being addressed directly.

She stammered and fell all over herself and finally said, "Oh, yes, I met him just the other day on the A train to Coney Island."

The hostess and all the guests were mortified; it took them a few minutes to regain their composure. But eventually, the hostess found her tongue again and smoothed things over by chattering with her other guests.

After all the good-byes were said and Florrie was in the car with Yonkel, the husband lashed out at her. "I thought I told you to keep quiet!" he shouted. "You embarrassed me beyond belief, I hope you know that."

Florrie was crestfallen. Yonkel continued. "My God," he ranted, "There wasn't a single person there who didn't know that the A train does not go to Coney Island!"

Beating the Rap

One member of a congregation said to another, "Our rabbi is such a good man. He lives very sparingly on his meagre salary; and he won't accept payment for any special services he performs for any member of the congregation. He won't even accept a gratuity for performing a marriage."

"Yes," agreed the other. "As a matter of fact, the man would probably starve to death except for one thing: every Monday and Thursday he fasts!"

MR. AND MRS. GOLDFINK were worried. All their friends' children had expressed their wishes about what they were going to grow up to be—firemen, policemen, whatever. But their little five-year-old had said nothing about a future career.

"I'll tell you what we'll do," said Mr. Goldfink. "We'll put him in a room, all alone, with only a Bible, an apple, and a silver dollar. If he reads the Bible, it means he's going to become a rabbi. If he eats the apple, he wants to be a farmer. And if he plays with the dollar, he's headed for banking."

So the parents put their boy into the room with the three items and waited half an hour. Then they went in to see what he was doing. He was sitting on the Bible, eating the apple, and had put the silver dollar in his pocket!

"What does that mean?" whispered Mrs. Goldfink to her husband.

"It means he's going to be a politician!"

AN OLD WOMAN living in New York died at the age of seventy-seven, leaving a grieving husband of sixty-eight years to survive her.

However, when a reporter came to interview the husband about their fifty years of marriage, he surprised him in the living room with the maid on his lap, his arms entwined around her.

"I can't believe my eyes," squawked the reporter. "After fifty years of marriage, and your wife hardly buried!"

The widower dropped his arms abruptly and did some fast thinking. "In my grief," he said finally, "do I know what I'm doing?"

Not My Problem

An old gent was going to the mountains for the first time in his life. He was poor, so he had to go by bus, but that didn't dent his spirit. He was so happy that he began singing as soon as he boarded the crowded vehicle.

The driver had been going for many hours, and wasn't too pleased about having the old man standing in the aisle right behind him, singing at the top of his lungs. And he told him so.

But the singing didn't stop; and after several vain exhortations, the driver warned the man that if he didn't cut out the singing, he'd stop the bus and toss out his valise. Even this threat didn't quiet the old man. Fifteen minutes later, the driver pulled off the road, walked up to the old man, picked up the valise, and threw it out the nearest window.

Then the driver returned to his seat. But the singing continued. Finally the driver listened to the words: "I'm going to the mountains! I'm going to the mountains! I won't call the police! I didn't bring a valise!"

REUBEN WAS SHOWING his West Coast cousin around his old New York neighborhood. "And that building over there," he said, "is a home for orphans."

"Now, Reuben," said the cousin, "I haven't been here for many years, but I'm sure that institution hasn't changed. I know that that building is an old-age home."

"Well," countered Reuben, "if you go inside, I'll bet you won't find a single person in there who isn't an orphan."

Think About It

Levy manufactured swimwear. Business was terrible. But Levy thought he saw a last chance to avoid bankruptcy by buying a huge lot of underwear at a very low price. If he could sell it all at a good profit, he'd be all right. So Levy borrowed several thousand dollars from his bank.

Unfortunately, the sales turned out to be slow. What was worse, his bank called him in to ask for the money. He had signed a demand note.

"Mr. Levy," said the bank president, "we'll have to call in your loan. We've no alternative."

"Well," said Levy, "are you yourself perhaps interested in underwear?"

The president laughed. "Mr. Levy, I am not in the least interested in the underwear business."

"Too bad," said Levy, "because as of this week, you're in it."

THE NEW NEIGHBOR joined the mah jongg group for the first time, and all the ladies gaped at the huge diamond she wore.

"It's the third most famous diamond in the world," she told the women confidentially. "First is the Hope diamond, then the Kohinoor diamond, and then this one—the Rabinowitz diamond."

"It's beautiful!" admired one woman enviously. "You're so lucky!"

"Not so lucky," the newcomer maintained. "Unfortunately, with the famous Rabinowitz diamond, I have received the famous Rabinowitz curse."

"And what is that?" wondered the women.

The woman heaved an enormous sigh. "Mr. Rabinowitz," she said.

IT WAS A BROILING day in July. Mrs. Finkelstein went into a store to buy a fan.

"What kind fan do you want?" asked Levy, the storekeeper. "We have fans for a nickel, for a quarter, and for a dollar."

"So give me one for a nickel," said Mrs. Finkelstein.

"O.K." said Levy, as he handed her a thin Japanese paper fan.

In 10 minutes, Mrs. Finkelstein was back. "Look what trash you sold me!" she shouted. "The fan broke."

"It did?" said Levy. "And how did you use it?"

"How did I use it?" replied Mrs. Finkelstein. "How do you use a fan? I held it in my hand, and I waved it back and forth in front of my face. Did you ever?"

"Oh no!" explained Levy, "With a five-cent fan, you got to hold it still, in both hands, like this, and wave your head back and forth in front of it."

ONE DAY, A BUTCHER accidentally cut his throat while shaving. The bleeding was so profuse, he fainted. He was carted off to the hospital.

When the butcher awoke, the nurse told him what had happened, and informed him that he wouldn't be able to eat for a while. But all he wanted to know was what his hospital stay would cost him. The nurse told him he was being charged $150 a day.

The man was furious that he had to pay so much and he wasn't even allowed to eat. He wanted his money's worth! So he demanded a glass of tea.

The nurse quietly went down the hall and got him a cup of tea. Then she returned and calmly injected the tea into the tube attached to the butcher's arm.

"Oy, Oy, Oy!" came the shouts.

"What's the matter?" the nurse asked. "Is the tea too hot?"

"No," yelled the butcher, "it's too sweet. How can I drink tea without lemon!"

Just Desserts

Max knelt mournfully at the bedside of his dying wife. Esther suddenly began speaking, but Max hushed her, saying, "Don't try to talk."

"Max, I have to talk," came the faint voice. "I must confess."

Max was crying openly now. "There is nothing to confess," he murmured through his tears.

"No, no, I must die in peace. I must confess. Max, I have been unfaithful to you."

Max laid a soothing hand on his wife's fevered cheek. "Now Esther, don't be concerned. I know all about it. Why else did I poison you?"

AFTER THE UNITED STATES launched its space program, the astronauts became overnight heroes. Everyone spoke of their accomplishments.

Two feisty Jewish ladies were indulging in their morning chat and one remarked, "Bessie, did you hear about the astronauts? I understand they went around the world several times!"

The other lady was not impressed. "Big deal!" she sniffed. "If you have money, you can afford to travel."

Quick Thinking

In the old country, there was a rabbi who traveled from village to village. In each town he would hold services, and then stay for several hours while the congregation offered him their simple fare and asked questions.

The rabbi's means of transportation was a

horse cart, driven by a sturdy, kindly fellow who admired the rabbi greatly. On every visit, after services, while the rabbi was being surrounded by the congregants, the driver would sit by patiently in the synagogue and listen.

After many years, the driver felt bold enough to ask the rabbi to grant one request. Just once, he'd like to feel the thrill of adulation. Wouldn't the rabbi trade places with him just once.

The rabbi wanted to please his loyal driver and granted the request.

The next day, the pair visited a new town. The rabbi and the driver exchanged garments. The rabbi quietly sat in the corner of the synagogue while the crowd gathered around the driver to feed him handsomely, and ask him questions. The driver handled the services and the questions very well for he had listened to his beloved rabbi for many years and he was entirely familiar with the stock questions.

Suddenly, a student arose and posed a complicated philosophical problem. The townsfolk turned to the driver, expecting a profound reply. But the driver knew he was stumped.

He hesitated for just a moment, and then he scoffed, "Young man, I am amazed that you should ask such a simple question. Why, even my driver, who is not well-versed in the Talmud, can answer that. And just to show you, we'll ask him!"

GOLDBERG WALKED INTO his partner's office at Goldberg and Cohen Dressmakers. "I have in my office an order from Marshall Field and Company in Chicago!" he exclaimed.

"I don't believe it," said Cohen.

"You don't believe it? Well, here, take a look at the cancellation."

MAX HAD BEEN SELECTED as an usher for the High Holy Day services at his synagogue and he took his duties seriously. He checked all tickets strictly, and wouldn't allow anyone in who didn't have one.

Suddenly Sammy Fishbein rushed up to him. "Max, I got to see my brother up front!"

"Where's your ticket?" asked Max.

"I don't have one," pleaded Sammy. "But I gotta see my brother! It's a matter of life and death!"

"All right," Max agreed, and stepped aside. "Go on in. But don't let me catch you praying!"

TWO LADIES LAY side by side on chaise lounges poolside at a swank Miami Beach hotel. One couldn't stop talking about her analyst. The other just lay prone and listened.

Finally, the listener entered the competition. "You ought to try *my* doctor. He's marvelous!"

Her companion asked, "Why should I see your doctor? There's nothing wrong with me."

"Oh!" replied the other, "My doctor's wonderful, he'll *find* something!"

A BEGGAR STOPPED a businessman and asked if he could spare a quarter.

The businessman drew himself up and asserted, "I don't hand out money on the street."

The schnorrer retaliated, "So what should I do? Open up an office?"

A Favor

A miserable young man, who despaired of ever finding happiness, drove to the end of a pier, with the intention of throwing himself into the river.

Suddenly, a policeman came running up to him, shouting, "Don't do it! Don't do it!"

The boy explained mournfully, "My girlfriend left me. I don't want to live any more. I just want to end it all!"

"Listen, mister," pleaded the Jewish cop. "If you jump, I'll have to go in after you and try to save you. But I don't know how to swim, and what are my wife and six kids going to do if I drown? Would you want that on your head? So, please, do me a favor and go home. In the privacy of your own home, go hang yourself."

Two FELLOWS MET at noon one day for lunch. One ordered chicken soup; the other, borscht.

The waiter brought one bowl of chicken noodle soup and one bowl of potato soup.

"I didn't have any more borscht," he said. "I brought you potato soup instead. Try it, it's good."

So the man tasted the soup and loved it. "It's great. The best I ever had!" And he offered some to his companion.

"It *is* good," said the other man. "Waiter, since it's so good, why didn't you bring *me* some potato soup?"

The waiter was offended. "Say, mister," he said, "did you order borscht?"

Consumer Reports

A clothing manufacturer repaired to the office of a marriage broker. He wanted to get married. The marriage broker asked his client exactly what he had in mind. The next day, the broker went out and found a lovely young thing that fit the bill perfectly.

The businessman looked at the photograph shown him, and said the girl seemed all right. But he wanted proof. "Before I buy goods from a mill I look at swatches; and before I get married, I must have a sample."

The broker was outraged. He insisted it couldn't be done, that a respectable young lady would have no part of such an approach. But the businessman was adamant. "That's the way it will be done, or it won't be done at all."

So the marriage broker went back to the girl and apologetically explained the situation. What did she want to do?

"I'm as smart in business as he is," answered the girl. "References, I'll give him. Samples, no!"

A MAN TOOK HIS FAMILY to a kosher restaurant. They were surprised when their waiter turned out to be Chinese! What's more, the Chinaman took their orders in Yiddish and even addressed them in Yiddish. The family was impressed.

When they had finished their meal, the man asked to see the manager.

"The food was excellent," he said. "I compliment you. But how did you get a Chinese waiter to talk Yiddish so well?"

"Shh!" said the proprietor. "Don't let him hear you. He thinks he's learning English!"

You Can't Fool Me!

Mr. Rosen had spent two weeks in New York City on business and was taking the train back to his suburban town. Sitting next to him on the train was a young man he didn't know. Since the train ride was long, Mr. Rosen decided to strike up a conversation.

"Where are you headed?" he asked.

The stranger smiled and said, "To Glens Falls."

Mr. Rosen was surprised. "Why, that's where I'm going! As a matter of fact, I live there! Is it a business trip?"

"No," said the young man, "it's social."

"Oh, do you have relatives there?"

"No, I don't."

Mr. Rosen thought a bit. "Are you married?" he asked.

"No, I'm not."

Now Rosen mused to himself. "He's going to Glens Falls, he's not married, it's not business, and he has no relatives there. So why is he going? Obviously, to meet a girl—to meet her family? Confirm their engagement? But who? There are only three Jewish families he could possibly know . . . the Resnicks, the Feldsteins, and the Sanowitzes.

"It couldn't be the Resnicks. Resnick has only sons. The Feldsteins have two girls, but one's married, and the other's in college and she wouldn't be home at this time of year. It must be the Sanowitzes. They have three: Marsha, Rebekkah, and Rochelle. Marsha is already engaged. Becky is too plump and unattractive for this nice-looking young man. So it must be Rochelle. Yes, Rochelle! She's beautiful!"

With this, Mr. Rosen broke his silence and smiled at the stranger. "Well, congratulations on your forthcoming marriage to Rochelle Sanowitz!"

"But—but how did you know?" stammered the young man.

"Why, it's obvious!" answered Mr. Rosen.

A SUCCESSFUL SELF-MADE MAN was at the bank one day when he ran into an old school chum. "Well, if it ain't my old pal Schlomo Walberg! How's by you?"

"Pretty good," said the friend. "By the way, I'm no longer Walberg. I changed my name to Eldridge."

The other man was surprised. "And where did you get the name 'Eldridge,' Schlomo?"

"What do you mean 'where?'" said the friend. "Don't you remember twenty years ago we both lived on Eldridge Street? Well, that's where I got the name. And what's more, I'm no more Schlomo. People now call me C.R."

His friend was even more curious. "And what does C.R. stand for?"

"C.R.—that stands for corner Rivington."

An 82-year-old woman tottered into Dr. Meyrowitz's office. "Doctor," she told her physician, "I'm not feeling too good."

"I'm sorry, Mrs. Kupnick, some things not even modern medicine can cure. I can't make you any younger, you know."

Mrs. Kupnick replied, "Doctor, who asked you to make me younger? All I want is for you to make me older."

Smart Finance

In the days of pioneering the old Wild West, Jake and Izzy were traveling through Colorado by stagecoach. Suddenly the coach stopped, and Jake realized that robbers were about to stage a hold-up.

Quickly, Jake took some money from his wallet and handed it to his companion. "Izzy," he explained, "here is the fifty dollars I owe you."

SAM WAS HOBBLING down the street when he met up with his old friend Moe.

"What's wrong, Sam?" asked Moe. "Why are you hobbling so?"

"*Why?*" complained Sam loudly. "Because my shoes are absolutely killing me!"

Moe was confused. "So why do you wear them?" he asked.

"Well, I'll tell you," sighed Sam. "My business couldn't be worse. I owe the butcher, the baker, the grocer, the landlord. I have two daughters so ugly who knows if I'll ever be able to get them married. My son is a slob, and my wife nags, nags, nags until I go crazy. I come home each night from a lousy day's work, and I look at the bills and at my family, and at that point I could kill myself.

"So I take off these damned shoes—and, Moe, that's the only pleasure I ever get!"

TWO MEN OF CHELM were having a debate: Which was the more important, the sun or the moon? One held that the sun, being larger and more powerful, was more important.

The other countered, "No! You're wrong! The moon is definitely more important than the sun. Without the light of the moon, our nights would be so dark we couldn't see a thing. The sun, on the other hand, shines by day—when it's light anyhow!"

A RUSSIAN JEW had become successful. He was allowed to travel outside the country as a member of the Russian embassy. In England, he met up with some young Jewish Socialists, and found himself subject to many questions.

"Comrade," said one of the Britishers, "I understand you are a Jew; I understand you are a man of integrity. Now it would be of great interest to me to have your opinion of the Soviet attitude toward the Arab-Israeli conflict. Why do the Russians support the Egyptian fascists against the democratic Israelis?"

The Russian said nothing.

But the questioners continued. "I know your country has an official policy, and so does your party. But as a Jew you must have your own view of justice. Who do you think is right?"

The Russian maintained his silence.

But the young Englishmen persisted. "Surely you have some opinion?" they demanded.

Finally the Russian, up against the wall, replied, "Yes, I do have an opinion, but I do not agree with it."

Look on the Bright Side

So many American Jews have been traveling to Israel recently, it is said that El Al, the Israeli airline, has instructed its crew members to learn Yiddish. One stewardess tells of the pilot who really caught the Yiddish idiom in all its flavor.

His message just after a New York take-off ran:

"*Shalom,* ladies and gentlemen, and welcome to El Al airlines. This is your pilot, Avi Goldberg, wishing you a happy; restful trip, which we certainly expect you to have, God willing. And if by some remote chance we do run into trouble—God forbid!—do not panic, keep calm. Your life belt is under your seat, and if you must put it on, wear it in good health!"

LITTLE HERBIE'S PARENTS decided he was of an age where they should start guarding their conversation.

When Aunt Dottie came to visit, she said to Herbie, "Well, young man, what's new around here?"

Herbie's reply was brief. "Who knows?" said the little boy. "They spell everything!"

MR. GOLD HAD BEEN married for many years when he had to go to Paris for a business trip. In that city of love, he easily fell victim to the amorous advances of the pretty mademoiselles.

But somehow Mrs. Gold found out about it. She wired her husband at his hotel: "COME HOME! WHY SPEND MONEY THERE FOR WHAT YOU CAN GET HERE FOR FREE?"

The next day, she received a cable in reply: "I KNOW YOU AND YOUR BARGAINS!"

MAX WAS CONVERSING with Sam about the synagogue they went to. "Sam," he said, "rabbis have a pretty easy life, don't they? They pray, they preach, and they make good money for that. Besides, comes a wedding or a funeral and they get a hefty fee."

"Well," replied Sammy, "I'll tell you what my father used to say. The rabbi gets the fees, but it's the *mohel* who gets the tips!"

Play It Again, Sam

A West Coast businessman had arranged to secure tickets to a Carnegie Hall concert during the week of his business trip to New York.

Killing time, he wandered about the streets of New York. Suddenly he realized he had no idea where Carnegie Hall was. So he stopped at a Jewish delicatessen and asked a waiter, "How do I get to Carnegie Hall?"

"Practice! Practice!" answered the waiter.

MR. BERNARD I. FEINBERG was a wealthy man who had been so busy all his lifetime making money, he'd never had time to attend synagogue. When he died, it was hard for the family to find a rabbi willing to speak at his funeral, for Feinberg had been an uncommonly unpleasant man.

Finally, a rabbi from outside the community was engaged. When the rabbi saw how well off the Feinbergs were, he presumed the best about the deceased and delivered a beautiful eulogy.

As the praise flowed on, Mrs. Feinberg looked up in surprise, and poked her brother in the ribs. "For God's sake, Max," she said, "Take a look inside the coffin and see if it's Bernie in there!"

Driving A Hard Bargain

Abe Seltzer was passing a golf course when he was struck in the head by a golf ball.

Seething, Abe picked up the ball and gestured wildly at the player running anxiously toward him. "I'll sue you in court for five hundred dollars!" Abe shouted angrily.

The golfer tried to excuse himself. "I hollered 'Fore!'" he said.

"All right!" answered Abe, "I'll take it."

Two old friends met, after not having seen each other for years. "Rosie! You look marvelous!" exclaimed Gussie.

"Yeh," said Rosie, "I'm feeling great. I'll tell you a secret. I'm having an affair."

Gussie smiled broadly. "Oh, that's marvelous! Who's catering?"

Lox

A schnorrer made his monthly call at Baron Rothschild's mansion and begged to be seen by the master. Admitted to the library, the schnorrer asked the tycoon to give him double his regular stipend, spilling out a heart-rending tale of woe.

Rothschild was moved, and gave the beggar what he had asked for. Yet the baron was suspicious, and commanded a servant to follow the poor man to see what he did with the money. The beggar headed for a swank delicatessen shop and spent the money on a lox.

The next month when the schnorrer came again to ask for more money, Rothschild erupted in anger.

"You scoundrel!" he cried, "What a trumped up hard luck story you handed me! As soon as you left my house last month, you went and spent the entire sum of money I gave you on lox!"

The schnorrer looked pitiful. "Ah, Baron,"

he replied, "put yourself in my position. When I haven't got money, I can't buy lox. When I have money, I can't buy lox. Tel me, your honor, when can I buy lox?"

THE PRESIDENT of the congregation had to undergo surgery. The board met to decide how to show their concern. Finally, it was agreed that the secretary of the congregation would visit the president in the hospital.

Two days after the operation, the secretary visited the sickroom. "I bring you the good wishes of our board," he said. "We hope you get well and live to be 120 years old!"

The president smiled back weakly.

"And that's an official resolution," continued the secretary, "passed by a vote of twelve to nine."

SOL TURNED TO MANNY and exclaimed in exasperation, "Ah, Manny, tell me, what can I do with that son of mine? The boy doesn't know how to drink, and he doesn't know how to play cards."

Manny was surprised. "What's the problem, Sol? That doesn't sound bad to me. Why do you complain?"

"Because," replied Sol, "he drinks and he plays cards!"

MAX SAT IN a restaurant waiting for his meal. He tapped a passing waiter on the arm. "Excuse me, what time is it?"

"Sorry," came the reply, "where you're sitting is not my table."

That's Progress!

Mr. Rosenberg was eighty years old and he'd spent all of his life in New York City. His family decided that this particular winter he should have a change. He should fly to Miami and stay in a ritzy hotel.

"But I don't want no ritzy hotel!" Mr. Rosenberg protested. "It won't be kosher. And I won't eat in a place that's not kosher!"

But the family reassured him, "For heaven's sake, so many Jewish people go to Miami, you don't think the hotels there are kosher? We'll find you a place that is guaranteed kosher."

So they found a place; and with misgivings, Mr. Rosenberg boarded the plane for Miami. The hotel manager, informed of the old man's concerns, met Mr. Rosenberg at the airport and took him to the hotel. Showing him the various facilities before he took him up to his room, the manager explained, "We have card playing every afternoon, movies twice a week, a TV set in every room—"

Mr. Rosenberg interrupted. "But your kitchen," he asked, "is it *absolutely* kosher?"

"Of course!" said the manager emphatically. He showed Mr. Rosenberg up to his room.

The old man stopped at the door and automatically reached up to touch the *mezuzah* (door amulet). But there wasn't any!

"No *mezuzah*?" cried Mr. Rosenberg.

"Don't be upset," smiled the manager. "On the roof, we've installed a master *mezuzah*."

It Could Be Worse

Two garment manufacturers met in the bank one Friday morning.

"So, Stanley," said one, "how's business?"

The other man just shrugged. "Ehhh," he said.

The first one smiled. "Well, for this time of the year, that's not bad!"

Fish Story

Mrs. Shapiro went into the delicatessen and asked for a nice smoked fish. The man brought her a large salmon. Mrs. Shapiro eyed it suspiciously. Something told her it wasn't too fresh. She then leaned over and began whispering to it.

"Lady!" exclaimed the counterman, "What are you doing?"

"Why, I'm talking to this fish," she answered.

"Talking to a *fish*?" The man was amazed.

"Certainly," said Mrs. Shapiro. "I happen to know seven fish languages."

"What did you say?"

"Oh, I asked this salmon where he was from, and he answered, 'From Peconic Bay.' So I asked him how things are in Peconic Bay, and he answered, 'How should I know? It's been years since I was there!'"

IZZY DECIDED TO BUILD himself a swimming pool in his backyard.

Several days later one of Izzy's neighbors came by and asked him if he'd gotten a permit to build the pool.

"Permit? What permit? I don't need no permit to build a pool in my own backyard."

The neighbor was sure that Izzy did, but Izzy pooh-poohed it all, and forgot about it.

When the pool was almost finished, a city

official appeared. "We've received a complaint," said the official, "and I see that it is justified. You failed to apply for a permit to build this pool."

"I didn't know you had to have permission," Izzy alibied.

"Indeed, you do," said the official. "There are zoning laws, and a project like this must be approved in advance. You can build a decorative pool or a fish pool without permission, but not a swimming pool."

"Well," smiled Izzy, "in that case, this is a fish pool."

"Come, come," sighed the official. "This is too big for a fish pool. And if this really is to be used for a fish pool, why did you install a filter?"

"Because," answered Izzy, "this is a gefilte fish pool."

This Is Not the Worst

Two neighborhood cronies were gossiping one morning when a third lady eagerly joined the group.

"Have I got a story!" interrupted the newcomer. "Poor old Linsky just tripped at the top of the stairs, fell down to the bottom, hit his head, and died."

"Died?" exclaimed the other ladies.

"Yes," asserted the talebearer. "And he broke his glasses, too."

AT A DINNER PARTY, the hostess served the appetizers herself, carrying the tray around to each guest. One man, however, declined.

"But you must!" insisted the lady.

"Really, they're delicious," replied the guest, "but I've had six already."

"Actually, you had seven," advised the hostess, "but who's counting?"

MRS. KOHANSKY WENT to her butcher of many years and said, "Bernie, today I need a beautiful chicken, maybe four pounds."

Bernie pointed out three chickens in the display counter, but Mrs. Kohansky turned up her nose at all of them. "I asked for a *beautiful* chicken," she sniffed.

So Bernie went to the back of the store, and

from his refrigerator room he extracted an especially plump fowl. He brought it forward with pride.

The lady was cautious. She took the chicken and slowly began to examine each part with her fingers—lifting the wings, feeling the breast, and groping inside the cavity.

Finally, the butcher's patience waned. "Tell me, Mrs. Kohansky," he demanded, "do you think *you* could pass such a test?"

It Would All Work Out

The grocer's son had come home from his first year at the university and was anxious to discuss serious subjects with his father. The grocer was pleased.

"Father," the idealistic young man expounded, "it seems to me the world is crazy. The rich, who have lots of money, buy on credit, but the poor, who don't have a cent, must pay cash. Don't you think it should be the other way around? The rich, having money, should pay cash; and the poor, having none, should get credit."

The grocer smiled at his son's lack of business acumen. "But," he pointed out, "if a storekeeper gave credit to the poor, he himself would soon become poor."

"So what?" countered the college boy. "Then he would be able to buy on credit, too!"

A WEALTHY MAN decided to eat his lunch in the park one day to catch some rays of sun. Suddenly, an old man appeared, dressed in rags.

"Mister," entreated the poor man, "I haven't eaten anything for three days."

The rich man kept on eating.

"It's three days, mister, that I haven't eaten."

Still no response.

The beggar made still another try. "You hear—three days that no food has passed my lips."

The rich man was quite obviously annoyed as he put down his sandwich. "It's amazing. You yourself won't eat, yet you won't let me eat either."

Why Take a Loss If You Don't Have To?

Two Scotsmen and a Jew gathered at the casket of a friend. The first Scotsman made a little speech.

"As you well know, my friends, I am a thrifty soul, but there is a legend in my family that if one places a wee bit of money in the casket to be buried with the body, it will ease the departed's way into the next world. For the sake of our friend, I place ten dollars in the casket with him."

The second Scotsman didn't want to look cheap, so he, too, took out a ten-dollar bill and dropped it into the casket.

Then the Jew moved forward. "Do you think I won't join in this kind deed?" he asked. Whereupon he took out his checkbook and wrote a check for thirty dollars. He placed it in the dead man's hand, and took the two ten-dollar bills as change.

A Rose Is a Rose

Poor Mrs. Sanowitz! Her son had been feeling depressed so he'd gone to see a psychiatrist. And the doctor had told Walter that he had an Oedipus complex!

"What shall I do?" worried the saddened mother to her husband. Mr. Sanowitz was unsympathetic.

"Oedipus-Shmoedipus!" he said disdainfully. "So long as he loves his mother!"

WHEN TANNENBAUM GOT BACK from his vacation in Italy, he eagerly told his friends in the garment district all about it.

"I even was in a group that went to the Vatican," he said proudly. "And I got in to see the Pope!"

"The Pope!" One man was awed. "What did he look like?"

"Oh, he's a nice man. Thin and spiritual-looking. I figure a size 38, short."

TWO OLD RETIRED PROFESSORS sat on the front porch, rocking in their chairs.

"Ah," observed Mendel, "if I were Rockefeller, I'd be *richer* than Rockefeller."

"What do you mean?" asked Izzy. "How could that be?"

"Oh, I'd do a little teaching on the side."

THE TEACHER ENTERED her classroom in the school on Delancey Street and was horrified to find a small puddle on the floor right next to her desk.

"Who did this?" she demanded. No one spoke.

"I want to know who made this puddle," she said again. "Please raise your hand, whoever did it." Again, no child moved.

So she realized that the offender might be too embarrassed to confess and decided to try another tactic. She took a rag from the closet and left it on her desk. Then she said, "I'm going to leave the room for a few minutes. I want the person who made that puddle to clean it up while I'm gone."

She left the room, closing the door behind her, and after waiting five minutes, she again entered the classroom. But to her amazement, there were now *two* puddles near her desk! She was furious! Trying to compose herself and to figure out what to do next, she turned her back to the class and faced the blackboard.

And there, scrawled in big letters, she read: "The Phantom Pisher Strikes Again!"

It Runs in the Family

It was the first day of school and the teacher was anxious to get to know her class and have them learn about each other as well. So she suggested that as she called out each name, the child would stand at his seat and say any sentence that came into mind.

She started with Tommy Avery. Tommy stood and said, "I like to play baseball."

"Good," said the teacher. "Now John Bennett."

"I like the summertime because then I can go to camp."

"Harold Cohen."

"I pledge a hundred dollars."

Two ladies had taken a vacation together and were having a marvelous time. They shopped in the morning, relaxed by the pool in the afternoon, and now were getting ready for a sumptuous meal in the evening.

"How about a cocktail before dinner?" suggested one lady.

"No, thanks," said the other. "I never drink."

"No? Why not?"

"Well, in front of my children, I don't believe in taking a drink. And when I'm away from my children, who needs it?"

The Tailor

Mrs. Mandelbaum was on her way out of the supermarket when she ran into her old friend Mrs. Rosenstein. The ladies hadn't seen each other for years, so they had much to catch up on.

"Tell me," said Mrs. Rosenstein, "how's your boy David?"

"Oh, David!" cried Mrs. Mandelbaum. "What a son. He's a doctor with a big office!"

"Wonderful. And what about Benjamin?"

"Benny! He's a lawyer. He even might run for office next year!"

"Marvelous! And your third son, Mendel?"

"Well, Mendel is still Mendel. Still a tailor." Mrs. Mandelbaum sighed. "I tell you, if it wasn't for Mendel, we'd all be starving!"

A DRESS MANUFACTURER from New York's garment district had to make a business trip which took him through Egypt.

At the Egyptian customs check-in, an official frowned at the American. "Are you a Jew?" he asked.

"Of course not!" exclaimed the New Yorker nervously.

"Well, what is your religion?"

"Me? I'm a Seventh Avenue Adventist."

A MAN AND HIS WIFE came to the village rabbi. The woman poured out a long history of her misery at the hands of her husband. "I can't stand it!" she wound up with. "He's awful!"

The old rabbi took her hand and said, "You're right."

Next it was the husband's turn. His story was just as accusing. He complained tearfully about his wife's behavior, citing many misdeeds.

The rabbi patted the man gently on the back, and said to him, "You're right."

A student who had been permitted to listen to both interviews now approached the rabbi, and whispered, "How can it be, rabbi? You told her *she* was right, and now you tell him *he* is right. How can both of them be right?"

"Ah!" answered the rabbi. "You're right, too!"

I'd Like to Try!

Some years ago, two rabbis met for lunch. After conducting a heavy philosophical exchange, the two turned to lighter topics.

"So," said one, "what do you think? One of our boys got to marry that Elizabeth Taylor!"

"Oh!" snapped the other, "It won't last a year!"

The first rabbi sighed. "I should have such a year!"

A SUCCESSFUL BUSINESSMAN nostalgically revisited the scenes of his youth, his old ghetto neighborhood.

He spotted a bearded elder talking to a youngster and hurried forward to get close enough to listen. He strained to hear the oldster's words of wisdom. "Ah!" admonished the old man. "That's what you say to a grandpa? Drop dead?"

THE GREAT RABBI lay dying. Devoted students flocked to his home to offer their respects.

The rabbi's wife permitted only very old friends and close colleagues to come to his bedside. The visitors murmured words of high praise for their respected leader.

"So pious!" mourned one man, as he testified to the rabbi's devotion to God.

"So learned," grieved another, speaking of the rabbi's knowledge of the Torah.

"So charitable," said a third, speaking of the rabbi's generosity toward every one he encountered.

The great rabbi listened quietly and impassively to all the words of praise. Then suddenly he raised himself to speak. Everyone leaned close to hear the wise man's final words.

"Piety! Learning! Charity! Fine!" muttered the rabbi. "And about my great modesty, you have nothing to say?"

A SCHNORRER CAME to Mrs. Friedman's door to collect his weekly stipend. But Mrs. Friedman had spent her last dollar at the supermarket, so she told him, "I'm sorry, but I haven't a penny in the house. Come back tomorrow."

At that, the schnorrer became angry.

"Tomorrow?" he growled. "Mrs. Friedman, don't let it happen again. I've lost a fortune extending credit!"

HARRIET GOLD loved borscht. One day, she was spooning herself a bowl of borscht when her pal, Abie, came to call.

"Harriet, I'm sorry to be the bearer of bad news," said Abie, "but Harry just got hit by a truck." Harriet kept on spooning her borscht.

"I don't think you heard me, Harriet," repeated Abie more urgently. "Harry's just been killed!"

Harriet kept on drinking the borscht. "I heard, Abie! I heard! As soon as I'm finished drinking this borscht, will I let out a scream!"

Don't Get Me Excited

Mr. Feldstein had been a painter for thirty years and he knew his business. So when he painted the bedroom in the house where he was working, he told the lady that it wouldn't be dry until the next morning. Nevertheless, that night the woman's husband couldn't resist testing, and he left a big handprint on the bedroom wall.

The next day Mr. Feldstein came back to start working on the kitchen. Soon after he arrived, the lady of the house said, "Listen, Mr. Feldstein, come into the bedroom. I want to show you where my husband put his hand last night."

Mr. Feldstein sighed. "Please, my good Mrs.," he said weakly, "I'm an old man. If you want to tip me, better give me a glass of tea!"

BUSINESS WAS SO TERRIBLE in the garment district
that Horowitz decided he couldn't take it any
more. He was facing bankruptcy and utter
shame and ruin. Suicide was the only way out.

Taking the elevator from his sixth-floor
office all the way up to the twenty-fourth floor,
Horowitz said a mental good-bye to his wife
and his business partner Finkel. Then he
jumped.

As he fell past the fifteenth floor, he overheard the chairman of Macy's talking on the
phone. "We'll be looking for a lot of soft tex-
tured clothing next fall," he heard the chairman
say.

As Horowitz passed his own office on the
sixth floor, he yelled to his partner, "Finkel! Cut
velvet! Cut velvet!"

Too Many

A suburban lady entered an exclusive boutique to look for a hat. She tried on many, but none seemed to satisfy her. One was too large, one too wide, another too dressy.

Finally, the exasperated saleslady said sweetly to her, "I wish I had a dozen like you," and walked to the back of the store.

Another saleslady, who had overheard the remark, was puzzled. "Why on earth did you say that to that obnoxious customer?"

"Because," said the worn-out woman through gritted teeth, "I have a hundred like her, but I wish I had only a dozen!"

I wish I had 2 like him,

Blind Date

Stanley was already in his twenties and he had never had a date with a girl, so his older brother decided it was time to do something about it. He arranged a blind date for Stanley with a nice young girl who was just as innocent as Stanley. But Stanley was very nervous. His hands became clammy and his tongue felt stiff as marble.

"Help me, Mark. I don't know how to talk to girls. How can I be a good conversationalist like you?" asked Stanley.

Mark had some advice to offer. "Listen, Stan," he said, "I have a formula that never fails. Talk about family, food, and philosophy. Any of those topics is guaranteed to get a girl talking. Try it! I'm sure it'll work."

So Stanley went to meet the girl. She was pretty and shy. Stanley wanted very much to make a good impression. He thought of his brother's advice. First, he'd talk family.

"Tell me," he began nervously, "do you have a brother?"

"No!" came the girl's swift reply.

"Oh." Stanley was stymied, so he moved to the topic of food. "Do you like noodles?"

"No!" she said again.

But Stanley wasn't at a loss. He remembered his brother's advice. He'd talk philosophy. "Say," he said, "if you had a brother, would he like noodles?"

JAKE AND HIS NEIGHBOR SAMMY were both working on their lawns after supper. Sammy called over the fence, "Is it true, Jake, that your mother-in-law is not well?"

"Yes, that's so," said Jake.

"She's in the hospital, my wife tells me," continued Sammy.

"Yes," replied Jake.

"And for how long has she been in the hospital?"

Jake thought about it and then replied, "In three weeks' time, please God, it will be a month."

ON THE GOLF COURSE one morning, a braggart decided to impress his companion. "Irving, what do you think I earned last year?" he asked.

Irving didn't look up from concentrating on his grip. "Half," he said.

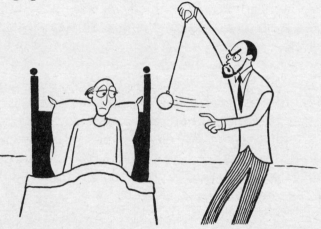

A Bedtime Story

Morris Bloomstein was upset. His father, a good man, was having trouble sleeping at night, and there was nothing the son could do to help. He gave the man ear plugs, pills, warm milk and honey, but nothing worked.

One day, Morris heard about a very expensive hypnotist who claimed he could suggest anything to a person's subconscious. He was especially noted for his work with insomniacs. So Morris called on the man, agreed to pay his huge fee, and made an appointment for him to come to the house.

The hypnotist came, and told Mr. Bloomstein to lie down on the couch. Slowly, he twirled his shiny watch before the man's eyes and spoke gently, softly, soothingly, watching the eyes begin to droop. "Relax, Mr. Bloomstein," he cooed. "Look at the gold watch—watch it move—you are getting sleepy—you are feeling heavy—so sleepy—you can't keep your eyes open—"

Mr. Bloomstein's eyes were closed now, and he was breathing smoothly and deeply. Morris, who was almost asleep himself, tiptoed out of the room with the hypnotist. He wrote him a large check, and showed him to the door with effusive thanks.

Then quietly he went back in to where his father lay peacefully. In the semidark room, Morris looked fondly on his father's relaxed face. Then suddenly, the man's eyes flew open and the voice was strong. "Well, Morris, has that crazy guy left already?"

AN ANTI-SEMITE CHALLENGED a Jew to a duel. At dawn, the next morning, the anti-Semite arrived at the appointed spot with his seconds. And they waited.

Half an hour later, the following message arrived from the Jew: "Unavoidably detained. Hate to disappoint you. So don't wait for me—go ahead and shoot."

"Hey, Moe, I hear you won the lottery! That's wonderful!" exclaimed Harry, as he clapped his friend on the back.

"Thanks, Harry," said Moe, "I guess sixty-three is just my lucky number."

Harry was curious. "Well, tell me, how did you happen to pick out a number like sixty-three?"

"I had a dream," explained Moe. "I dreamed I was in a theater, and on the stage was a chorus of sevens—each dancer a number seven, in a line exactly eight sevens long. So I chose sixty-three."

"But, Moe! Eight times seven is fifty-six, not sixty-three!"

"O.K., Harry, so *you* be the mathematician!" said Moe.

Mrs. Levy's son David had gone from New York, clear across the country to college in California. One day, David phoned his mother.

"Ma, I just got married," announced David.

"Wonderful, David! Mazel Tov!" said Mrs. Levy. "But what was so urgent about it that you had to get married in such a hurry and call me on the phone to break the news?"

"Well, Ma," said David, "there's a little problem. She's not Jewish."

"Oy vey!" shouted Mrs. Levy. But then she calmed down. "Well, I love you very much,

David. You're my only son and I guess I'll have to accept her and make the best of it."

"But there's another little difficulty, Ma," continued David. "She's a little older than I am. And also, she's pregnant."

"Oy, David!" screamed his mother. "How could you do such a thing?" But again she regained her control. "But you are my only son and I love you. I forgive you."

"Thanks, Ma, but there's still another little matter. She already has five children."

"David! David!" Mrs. Levy was distraught. "You're breaking my heart! But you're my own flesh and blood! What can I do for you?"

"Ma, we have nowhere to stay."

"Come to New York, David," said Mrs. Levy. "You can have this apartment."

"But, Ma, where will you stay?"

"Don't worry about me, David. As soon as I put down the phone, I'll drop dead."

Mind Your Own Business

A bearded old Jew entered a delicatessen and pointed to a slab of ham behind the glass counter. "A quarter pound of the corned beef, if you please."

The counter man noticed the beard and thought it his duty to inform the old man. "I'm sorry, sir," he said quietly, "but that's ham!"

"And who asked you?" retorted the elder.

IT WAS THE FIRST YEAR that the family had been living in Germany, and the father wanted his little boy to shine at his studies. Mr. Stein asked for Max's report card.

Reluctantly, Max showed it. Mr. Stein was angry, and scolded the boy for his poor grades.

"Well, Papa," said Max, "the other boys in my class are Nazis. They know I'm Jewish, and they bother me so that I can't study. That's why I got such a bad report card."

Mr. Stein relented. "All right, my son," he said. "Anything for your future. I'm converting you into a Nazi; then you won't have any more trouble."

So Max had no more trouble in his class. But at the end of the next term, he came home with another terrible report. Mr. Stein was furious. "What's your excuse now?" he yelled.

"Well," Max said, "You know, Papa, we Nazis don't learn as fast as those Jewish boys."

SAM WEINSTEIN AND Sol Applebaum owned a clothing factory and were quite pleased with the way business was going. One day, Sam decided that a well-to-do person ought to have a more elegant name. So he started calling himself Whittaker. And he changed the sign on the front of the factory from WEINSTEIN AND APPLEBAUM to WHITTAKER AND APPLEBAUM.

Sol was not to be outdone. He wanted to be

elegant, too. So he also changed his name to Whittaker. Now the sign in front of the factory read WHITTAKER AND WHITTAKER.

One morning, a prospective buyer came to call. "I'd like to see Mr. Whittaker," the man had said.

"Which one?" answered the receptionist, "Weinstein or Applebaum?"

It's Not Time Yet

Mrs. Heckstein was preparing dinner when a beggar came to her door. "Lady, I haven't eaten for three days. Have you got something for me?"

"I haven't got much," said Mrs. Heckstein. "Would you like maybe some noodle soup left from the night before?"

"That would be great!"

"Good! Then come back tomorrow."

FINKEL SPENT ALL MORNING trying to contact Saperstein and Shapiro, an important account. But when he asked for Saperstein, the secretary told him the man was out. And when he asked for Shapiro, the secretary told him he was tied up.

He'd called back five times, when he'd finally had enough. "What kind of business is this?" he fumed at the secretary. "One partner's out all morning, and the other's tied up for hours on end. What's going on there?"

The secretary apologized. "I'm sorry, Mr. Finkel, but, you see, whenever Mr. Saperstein goes out, he ties Mr. Shapiro up."

MR. AND MRS. LEIBENSTEIN had saved a lot of money and were traveling to a place they had always dreamed of—Hawaii.

But while on the plane to that exotic spot, the couple got into an argument over the pronunciation of the name. The wife insisted it was said with a "w"; the husband was sure the "w" was pronounced as a "v." They decided to ask a native as soon as they landed.

The plane pulled into the airport, the stairs were lowered, and the passengers debarked to the sounds of beautiful Hawaiian music being strummed for their welcome. Mr. and Mrs. Leibenstein approached one of the musicians and asked him, "Do you pronounce your island

'Hawaii' or 'Havaii'?"

"Havaii," said the man.

"Well, thank you," said Mr. Leibenstein, and he smiled smugly.

"You're velcome," said the musician.

She Knows Herself

A butcher was going over his account books and found that Mrs. Levy owed him a sizable sum of money. He called her on the phone several times, but could never get in touch, so he decided to send her a letter.

"Dear Mrs. Levy," he wrote, "please pay up the money that you owe me."

The next week, he received a reply in the mail: "I can't pay right now, but please send me two good chickens, four pounds of hamburger, and six steaks."

The butcher was angry. He wrote again: "Dear Mrs. Levy: I will send your order when you pay up your account."

The reply came the next day: "I can't wait that long!"

THE YOUNG SON of a garment maker was in school one day when the teacher asked him to name the four seasons.

The boy stood up and said, "I only know two: busy and slack!"

Mrs. Fein met Mrs. Schultz in the street one day and exclaimed, "Mrs. Schultz, how nice to see you again. But, you know, I hardly recognized you. What happened with your hair?"

Mrs. Schultz sighed and explained, "My hair was falling out of my head by the handful. So I went to the doctor but he told me he couldn't do nothing for me. The best thing, he told me, was I should get myself a wig. So that's the story."

But Mrs. Fein was immediately reassuring. "Mrs. Schultz, don't worry yourself a minute. No one would ever know."

It Never Hurts to Be Careful

Izzy was driving through the countryside when he became very thirsty. So in the next town, he looked for a coffee shop. But he found only a general store that was a combination hardware store, drugstore, and farmers' supply outlet all in one. Still, it boasted a soda fountain, so Izzy went in.

At the counter, he asked boldly, "Do you handle fertilizer here?"

"Why, yes," said the man, "I'll be glad to show you—"

"Never mind!" interrupted Izzy. "Just wash your hands, and make me a malted!"

Stick to Your Own Occupation

A beggar came every week to beseech a wealthy philanthropist for charity. Every week the rich man listened to his tale of woe and doled out a generous gift.

One day, the philanthropist took the beggar aside and said to him, "Listen, you know I will continue giving you a nice amount every week. You don't have to convince me any more. A little less cringing, a little less whining about your condition, and we would both be happier."

The beggar drew himself up and retorted frostily, "My good sir, I don't teach you how to be a millionaire; and please don't you teach me how to be a *schnorrer*" (beggar).

Outfoxing the Fox

During the Inquisition, the persecuted Jews had many opportunities to sharpen their wits. The story is told of a learned rabbi who was summoned before an ecclesiastical court. He was told that there were two pieces of paper in a box: one read "Innocent"; the other read "Guilty." The words would determine the fate of the Jews in town. The inquisitors ordered the rabbi to draw one of the papers blindly; the future of the Jewish people of that town was to be entirely in the hands of God. If He led the rabbi to draw the paper which said "Innocent," the Jews would go unharmed. That would be God's will. If he drew the paper that said "Guilty," all the leaders of the Jewish community would be executed, for that would be God's will.

The rabbi knew the inquisitor to be an unscrupulous man, and surmised that the word "Guilty" had been written on *both* slips of paper. He thought quickly. He selected one of the papers, and quickly swallowed it.

"What are you doing?" cried the judges. "How will we know what it said?"

"Very simply!" answered the rabbi. "Just look at the piece of paper left in the box. If it reads 'Innocent,' then the one I swallowed must have read 'Guilty.' But if the paper remaining in the box reads 'Guilty,' then the paper I swallowed obviously must have contained the word 'Innocent'!"

THE STUDENTS attending an international university were asked to write papers dealing with the elephant in any way they chose.

A German student wrote a fifty-page paper, called *An Introduction to the Study of the Elephant*. He also had thirty extra pages of footnotes and bibliography.

A French student handed in a short, beautifully lettered work, entitled *The Elephant and His Love Life*.

A British student created an illustrated travel guide, and he titled it *Hunting the Elephant in Deepest Africa*.

An American student wrote a paper which he called *How to Raise Elephants in Your Backyard for Fun and Profit*.

And the Jewish student wrote a paper on *The Elephant and Anti-Semitism*.

SAMMY WAS SITTING with his grandfather, having a glass of tea. The old man drank slowly, sipping the tea through the lump of sugar between his teeth. Then he put the glass down and heaved a deep sigh.

"You know, Sammy," he muttered. "Life is like a glass of tea." And he fell silent.

Sammy waited for him to continue, but he didn't. Finally Sammy prompted him, "Grandpa, why is life like a glass of tea?"

His grandfather shrugged, "And how should I know? What am I, a philosopher?"

Southern Romance

Fred Tannenbaum was stationed in a small Southern town. There he met a girl and fell madly in love. He called his mother to tell her he wanted to get married. Yes, the girl was Jewish.

"But you must be married by a rabbi!" insisted Mrs. Tannenbaum.

"There aren't any rabbis around here!" said Fred.

"I'll send you one!"

And so Mrs. Tannenbaum set off for her Lower East Side shul. She pleaded with her old rabbi to go South with her to marry her son. And he agreed. For the occasion, the rabbi put on his best beaver hat, his favorite black silk wedding suit, and his long black frock coat that almost touched the ground.

When they got off the plane, Mrs. Tannenbaum showed the cab driver the girl's address, but somehow or other he dropped them at the wrong place and drove off. Mrs. Tannenbaum, with the rabbi in tow, walked up and down the streets searching for Freddie and his bride-to-be. And as they went along, they seemed to attract a growing following. By the time they found the right address, there were a dozen people behind them staring at the rabbi.

The rabbi pulled himself up to his full height and faced the crowd of gaping Southerners. "What's the matter?" he said. "Ain't you never seen before a Yankee?"

MR. AND MRS. MANDELBAUM decided the only solution to their marital problems was in divorce. So they went to see the rabbi.

The rabbi was concerned about the three children and was reluctant to see the family broken up. He thought that if he could stall the couple maybe they would work it out together.

"Well," said the rabbi, "there's no way of dividing three children. What you'll have to do is live together one more year. You'll have a fourth child, and then, it will be easy to arrange a proper divorce. You'll take two children, and he'll take two."

"Nothing doing," said Mrs. Mandelbaum. "Rabbi, if I depended on him, I wouldn't even have had these three!"

Mrs. Markowitz was anxious because it was the first day her little boy was going to leave her and go to school. She tried hard to appear calm, but she couldn't hide the concern in her voice as she talked to her son that morning.

"So, my *bubeleh*, today you're starting to get grown up, you're going off to school, eh? And, *bubeleh*, you'll be a good boy and do whatever the teacher tells you to, yes? Now, you'll get nicely dressed up in your new suit, *bubeleh*, and you'll play at recess with the other children, but you won't mess up your new suit, will you, my *bubeleh*? And *bubeleh*, you'll come right home after school, okay?"

"Yes, mama," said the little boy, and he went off to school.

All day, Mrs. Markowitz sat waiting and worrying. At three o'clock she was at the door waiting for her boy. "So, my *bubeleh*! How was your first day of school? What did you learn? Tell your mama everything!"

"Well," said the boy, "I learned one thing. I learned that my name is not *bubeleh*, it's Irving!"

"Why didn't you ever get married?" Max asked his bachelor friend Sam during a rare heart-to-heart talk.

"Well, I thought of marrying several times," said Sam, "but each time something went wrong. The first time I was engaged, I was madly in love with the girl. She was sweet and educated and very charming. But my mother didn't like the way she looked, so I broke it off.

"Then I fell for another girl. She seemed to me to be the type that my mother would like, so I brought her home. Her looks were okay, but my mother didn't like the way she talked. So that was the end of that.

"And last year, I met a girl up in the mountains that I was sure my mother would adore. She looked like my mother, she dressed like my mother, she even talked like my mother. But when I brought her home, again I found out it couldn't be."

"Why?" asked Max. "Your mother didn't like her?"

"Oh, my mother liked her well enough," replied Sam. "But my father hated her!"

Giving Credit Where It's Due

After performing beautifully at his Bar Mitzvah, and listening to words of praise from the rabbi, and accepting a certificate from the Women's Auxiliary of the synagogue, young Harold was called upon to say a few words.

"For making this Bar Mitzvah day possible," began Harold, "I would like to thank my parents, my beloved teacher, Mr. Greenberg, our dear rabbi, Dr. Hochstein, and my psychiatrist, Dr. Leonard Winkowitz."

SADIE SAT BY the swimming pool at the Miami hotel. The two ladies beside her were discussing where they had their diamonds cleaned. One used a swank shop on Fifth Avenue; the other used someone in the Diamond Exchange that she had patronized for years; she found his small establishment prompt and reliable.

Then they turned to Sadie. Where did she have *her* diamonds serviced, they wanted to know.

Sadie thought quickly. "Oh, I don't worry about things like that," she said. "Whenever a diamond of mine gets dirty, I just throw it away!"

A GROCER HAD SUFFERED a heart attack and was carried upstairs to his apartment. Now, pale and weak, he knew there was no hope. The doctor said it would be only a matter of minutes.

"Are you there, Molly?" asked the man softly. His sorrowful wife pressed his hand.

"And Bernard, are you there?" he went on faintly.

"Yes, Father," came his son's reply.

"And Marsha, you're there?"

"Yes, Father," wept his daughter.

Then the grocer's voice came out full force. "You're all here, so who's minding the store?" he growled.

You Can't Get Everything

A matchmaker told a young man that he had the perfect girl for him. "She's a redhead!" he exclaimed with pride.

"You mean Becky, the tailor's daughter?" cried the young man.

"That's her!" beamed the matchmaker.

"You're crazy! She's almost blind!"

"That bothers you? That's a blessing; half the time she won't be seeing what you're doing."

"But she also stutters!"

"That's also a blessing. A woman who stutters will be afraid to speak, so you'll live a peaceful life."

"But she's deaf!"

"*I* should have such luck! With a deaf wife you can shout, you can scream as much as you want to."

"But she's twenty years older than I am!"

"Ah," retorted the matchmaker disgustedly. "I bring you a woman with such gifts, and you pick on one little fault!"

Two school chums met accidentally after many years of separation. Wishing to catch up on each other's lives, they decided to have lunch together.

"Well, so what's doing with your family?" asked the first. Proudly, the other man explained that his first son had become a surgeon, his second had become a prominent lawyer, and his third had gone into business and become president of a national corporation. "And what of *your* family?" he asked his friend.

The first man said, beaming, "I only had one son, but he became a rabbi."

"A *rabbi*?" replied his friend incredulously. "What kind of a career is that for a Jewish boy?"

Abe was on his way to the Coast when his train was derailed and fell into a ravine. All around him, passengers lay dead; he couldn't see a sign of life anywhere, but miraculously he himself was unhurt. However, he couldn't find a single door or window through which he could extricate himself. He was stuck in the car in danger of suffocation. After several hours, a rescue crew arrived and started breaking through a window to reach him.

"We're from the Red Cross," they announced.

Abe waved them off, "I gave already at the office."

Misunderstanding

Two bankers, Morris and Harry, decided to take a vacation together and get away from it all. They rented a cabin on a lake so they could go fishing.

The first morning of their vacation, the pair got into the boat and made their way out into the middle of the lake. Suddenly a large motorboat sped by, and the force of its wake caused the smaller craft to capsize.

"Help me, Morris! I can't swim very well." shouted Harry.

Morris could swim, but the problem was that Harry was twice his size. He'd never be able to rescue him. So he hollered, "I'll go get help. Do you think you can float alone?"

Harry was indignant. "Morris, how can you talk about business at a time like this?"

SAM GOLDSTEIN had never been to a show in the legitimate theater. For his birthday, his children decided to give him a present of a ticket for the Jewish theater.

The night after the show, they came to visit him and asked him eagerly what he thought of the show. "Ach," he answered, "it was simply nonsense. When she was willing, he wasn't willing. And when he was willing, she wasn't willing. And when they both were willing, down came the curtain."

A SIXTH-GRADE TEACHER was testing her class on vocabulary.

"Abie, can you tell me what a stoic is?" she asked.

Abie stood respectfully at his place. "A stoic," he said, "is the bird that brings the babies."

A RABBI, A PRIEST, and a minister were playing poker. Suddenly, the police burst into the room. "Sorry, gents, but gambling's illegal," said one of the officers, and he hustled the religious trio down to the court.

"I'm sorry about this," said the judge, "but now that you're here there's only one thing to do. Since you're all men of the cloth, I think I can trust your word. So I'll ask you if you were gambling, and whatever you answer, I'll believe you. We'll start with you, Father."

"Your Honor, surely it is important to be certain that we define what we mean by gambling. In a narrow, but entirely valid sense, what we describe as gambling is only truly so if there is a desire to win money, rather than merely to enjoy the suspense of the fall of cards. In addition, we might confine gambling to situations where the loss of money would be harmful, as—"

"Okay, Father," the judge interrupted. "I see that in the manner in which you define the word, you were not gambling. Now how about you, Reverend?"

The minister said, "I entirely agree with my learned colleague."

"Fine," said the judge. "And now you, rabbi. Were you gambling?"

The rabbi looked at his two friends, and then back at the judge, and asked, "With whom, Your Honor?"

The Signs of Civilization

A Jewish soldier stationed in Berlin got into a discussion with a German who was espousing the superiority of the Aryan.

Finally, the soldier had enough. "Listen, you big mouth," he cried, vehemently, "when your people were still in the woods eating acorns, our people already had diabetes!"

BORIS TOMASHEFSKY was probably the best-known actor on the Jewish stage. He really packed them in.

One night, during a performance toward the end of his career, Tomashefsky failed to appear for the third act. An announcer came to the stage and said, "Ladies and gentlemen, I have very sad news for you. Mr. Tomashefsky has just suffered a heart attack and cannot continue."

A voice from the gallery cried out, "Give him an enema."

The announcer then stepped forward, closer to the audience, and said, "My dear sir, perhaps you have not understood. Mr. Tomashefsky has just passed away."

Again the voice rang out, in raucous tones, "Give him an enema."

The announcer then said, "I know it's very shocking news, and I'm very sorry to have to be the one to announce it. But Mr. Tomashefsky is dead. Your suggestion could not possibly help him."

And the voice shot back, louder and more insistent, "Can't hurt."

Mistaken Identity

Izzy thought he saw his friend Tannenbaum walking up ahead of him on the street, so he quickened his pace and clapped the man soundly on the back. "Tannenbaum! I haven't seen you in a long time!" he cried.

Startled, the man turned around. He wasn't Tannenbaum at all. And he was pretty irritated at being thumped on the back. "My name is not Tannenbaum!" he fairly shouted. "And what's the idea of giving me such a hard slap?"

Izzy retreated icily. "What business is it of yours what I do to Tannenbaum?"

GOTTLIEB'S SECRETARY reported that the lady from the charity organization had called for the fifth time that morning. She couldn't say he was "in conference" still another time. So Gottlieb relented and took the call.

"See here, Mr. Gottlieb," asserted the high-powered voice, "we have asked you time and again for a contribution, and you've refused every time. Yet you have three homes, four elegant cars, you own a chain of department stores, and belong to two country clubs. So how can you turn us down?"

Gottlieb's tone was equally strong. "Madam, have you any idea of the situation in my family? My mother has a heart disease so severe she must remain in the hospital. My brother is indigent and on relief. My aged uncle is a cripple who can't support himself. So," Gottlieb continued, "if I don't give any of them any money, why should I give anything to you?"

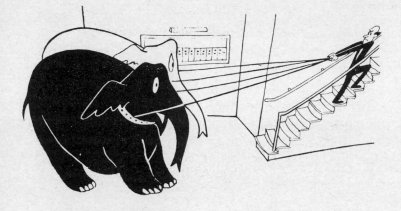

The Bargain Maven

Danny was an inveterate bargain hunter. He hadn't a penny to his name, but whenever he saw a bargain he couldn't resist it.

One day a friend of his came to see him. Jim said, "Danny, I've got a terrific bargain for you. A boatload has arrived for the Barnum and Bailey Circus and they have an overstock. They've got an elephant on board, a baby elephant, that's worth at least $2,000 and I can land it for you for only $300."

Danny looked at Jim as if he were half crazy. "What! An elephant! An elephant in my one-room apartment? You must be out of your mind! In the first place, there's no room for it. And in the second place, how could I feed it? In the third place, what could I do with it? Don't be nuts!"

"But," persisted Jim, "I'm telling you this

elephant is worth 2,000 bucks and I can get it for you for a mere 300, maybe even for 250."

Danny was adamant. "Get the hell out of here, will you? You're off your rocker. I don't need an elephant. I don't want an elephant. Leave me alone with elephants."

But Jim knew his friend and he continued hammering away. "Listen, Danny," he said, "the fact is they have an overstock. You know, I think if I put it to 'em I could get you two elephants for the same 200 bucks."

"Now you're talkin'," said Danny.

MINNIE AND MAX had been married for 18 years. As Minnie grew older and less attractive, Max became disinterested and his libido started to wane dramatically. In desperation, Minnie hauled him before a marriage counselor. The marriage counselor listened patiently to Minnie's complaints and to Max's protestations. Max said he was being nagged unmercifully; Minnie said that Max was causing her anguish.

Finally the marriage counselor issued a verdict. "Max," he said, "from now on, no matter how you feel, you must give Minnie her conjugal rights at least semi-annually."

Minnie was delighted and they left the counselor's chambers. On the way downstairs she nudged Max, "Tell me Max, how many times a week is semi-annually?"

THE TEACHER IN A tenement district sent Mrs. Cohen a candid note which read:

"Your son Abie stinks. Give him a bath."

Mrs. Cohen's reply was just as direct. "My son Abie ain't no rose. Don't smell him. Learn him."

MRS. GOLD FELL ASLEEP quickly one night, but her husband lay awake tossing and turning. Finally the commotion awoke Mrs. Gold, and she began complaining.

"Harry, what is it? Why are you tossing and turning so, that I can't even get a good night's sleep?"

"Oh, sweetheart," sighed Mr. Gold, "I'm so worried, that's what it is. I borrowed $3000 dollars from Jake Stein across the street, and I thought business was going to get better, but it's worse. The note is due tomorrow, and I've no idea where I'm going to get the money to pay it with."

"Is that what's keeping you awake?" asked Mrs. Gold. And with that, she opened up the window and started screaming, "Jake! Jake!"

In half-a-minute, Jacob Stein was at his window. "What's the matter?" he yelled back.

"Jake," yelled Mrs. Gold, "Abie owes you three grand. The note is due tomorrow. He's been up all night worrying where to get the money, but he can't raise it. Now *you* worry!"

MR. FELDSTEIN HAD gone to shul faithfully twice a day ever since his bar mitzvah. Every morning he lay *tfillin*. He had consulted God every time he took a new apartment, every time he had to decide on a name for a child, every time he had a problem with his business.

Yet when he turned 65, he was still a poor man. What was worse, his brother-in-law had never even come near a synagogue, and yet he was a millionaire! Mr. Feldstein couldn't understand it. So once more he went to God.

"Oh, God, have I not come to you with every event in my life? Am I not your obedient servant? Yet you make Morris a millionaire and me you make a poor man? Oh God, why is this?"

A sigh came up from the altar. Slowly the voice of God came in heavy tones. "Because, Feldstein, you're such a nudnick! All you do is bother me!"

Family Background

A jewelry store on Fifth Avenue bore the gold-engraved letters, "S. Astor." Seeing the sign, a bejeweled passerby thought to herself, "I wonder if they are *the* Astors." So she went inside.

"Pardon me, sir," she asked the proprietor, "but are you the Boston Astors?"

The man was very polite. "No," he replied. "The Boston Astors are the Steinbergs; we're the Ecksteins!"

SAMMY STEPPED UP to his friend who sold hot dogs from a pushcart and said casually, "So, Morris, how's business?"

Morris was open with his friend. "Oh, business is pretty good. I even was able to put a thousand dollars into my savings account!"

Sammy was quick to try to take advantage of this opportunity. "So, Morris, could you lend me a hundred?"

Morris didn't hesitate. "I'm sorry, but I'm not allowed to."

"You're not *allowed* to? What do you mean by that?"

"Well, I made an agreement with the bank. They agreed they won't go into the hot dog business, and I agreed not to lend money."

Observing the Formalities

Susie Eisenberg came home for Thanksgiving vacation during her first year at college and announced she wasn't going back to school.

Astonished, her father demanded to know why.

"Well, Dad," she sobbed, "I'm sorry to tell you, but I'm pregnant."

Mr. Eisenberg was badly shocked. "This is terrible," he moaned. "Who is the father?"

The poor girl wrung her hands. "Well, Dad, as a matter of fact, it's difficult to say. I can't pinpoint the father."

At this, Mr. Eisenberg hit the ceiling. "What do you mean you don't know the father? Me and your mother, we are simple people; we don't know the proper way to be introduced. But you, you are educated! Don't you know how to ask 'With whom am I having the pleasure?'"

ESSIE AND GERT went to visit their neighbor Rosie, who had just come home from the hospital with her triplets.

"Oh, Rosie, it's wonderful!" sighed Essie. "Imagine having triplets! I hear it's pretty rare."

Rosie replied smiling, "Rare? The doctor told me it's practically a miracle! He told me triplets happen only once in one million, six hundred and eighty times!"

"My God!" cried Gert. "Rosie, when did you ever have time to do your housework?"

IT WAS AT A country fair. Onto a platform there strode a huge giant of a man. He grabbed a 500-pound barbell and, with ease, lifted it above his head. For his next feat, he kneeled under a piano on which heavy weights had been distributed and, after tensing his muscles, he slowly raised the piano aloft on his back.

The hawker then came forward and announced, "For his next feat Lionel Strongfellow will perform a unique stunt. Here is a lemon, an ordinary lemon, a fresh lemon. Lionel Strongfellow will squeeze every bit of juice out of this lemon using both hands. If anybody in this audience can squeeze another drop of juice out of this lemon after Lionel Strongfellow has handled it, we will award the lucky man a prize of $500."

Strongfellow then took the lemon and squeezed it into a pulpy mass. He kneaded it again and again with both hands until it seemed that there wasn't any juice left in it at all. Then, in response to the hawker's invitation, three powerful men from the audience came up and each in turn tried to extract a drop of juice out of the lemon. None succeeded.

The hawker asked, "Anyone else care to try?" A slight short man strode up to the stage. It looked like sheer folly, but the little fellow took the lemon, squeezed it, and out spouted a stream of juice.

The hawker gave the man the prize and

asked in amazement, "Tell me, sir, by what kind of legerdemain, by what kind of magic, by what kind of incredible strength were you able to get juice out of this lemon, where everyone else before had failed?"

The man looked up and said, "Well, I've had lots of experience. You see, I've been a collector for the United Jewish Appeal for 12 years."

Spreading His Wealth

Benny had worked as a tailor for many years. Came the time when he wished to retire, but his savings account was spare.

"Miriam," he confided to his wife, "I'm tired. I want to retire, but I don't know how we're going to afford it."

"Don't worry," said Miriam, "I have plenty of money." And she produced a bankbook with regular deposits stretching back the entire forty years of their marriage.

"Where did this come from?" cried Benny in amazement.

"Well," said Miriam softly, "every time, during the last forty years, that we made love, I put five dollars away."

Benny threw his arms around his wife, and impulsively cried out, "Oh Miriam! For heaven's sake, you should have told me. If I had only known, I would have given you all my business."

A Good Question

In Hitler's heyday, a Jew was cornered by two rough Nazi blackguards. They stood him up against a wall and asked him, "Well you, you tell us right now, who was responsible for the defeat of Germany in 1917?"

The collared Jew blurted out, "The Jews and the bicycle riders."

The SS men were nonplussed. One of them asked, "Why the bicycle riders?"

"Ah," answered their victim, "why the Jews?"

Two WOMEN MET again after many years and began exchanging histories. "Whatever happened to your son?" asked one woman.

"Oh, what a tragedy!" moaned the other. "My son married a no-good who doesn't lift a finger around the house. She can't cook, she can't sew a button on a shirt, all she does is sleep. My poor boy brings her breakfast in bed, and all day long she stays there, loafing, reading, eating candy!"

"That's terrible," sympathized the first woman. "And what about your daughter?"

"Oh, she's got a good life. She married a man who's a living doll! He won't let her set foot in the kitchen. He gives her breakfast in bed, and makes her stay there all day, resting, reading, and eating chocolates."

THE LIMOUSINE PULLED UP in front of one of New York's poshest hotels and the doorman sprang forward to hold open the car door for Mrs. Henrietta de Rothsberg. Immediately, Mrs. de Rothsberg called for half a dozen bellboys.

The boys came running, and the lady dispatched them one by one with her suitcases, hatboxes, and wig stands. When she came to the last one, she announced regally, "And you, you can carry my son Steven."

The bellboy was aghast. Steven was a teenager, and no scrawny chicken. "But, madam," he complained, "surely the young man can walk."

Mrs. de Rothsberg was adamant. "Of course he can walk!" she explained. "But, thanks be to God, he'll never have to."

A CRUISING SHIP was sailing near Iceland when the captain spied an iceberg right in his ship's path. He tried to steer around it, but found to his horror that something was wrong with the rudder. The ship wouldn't turn.

Maintaining his calm, the captain immediately wired for help, and ships and helicopters were dispatched. In the meantime, the captain tried to think of some way to keep the passengers from noticing the fearful peril ahead.

Then he remembered that there was a magician aboard. So he called the man in and explained the situation. "Please do a show for the passengers to keep them occupied," said the captain. "If it becomes unavoidable for us to hit the iceberg, I'll signal you. When you see me signal, just tell the audience that for your final act, you'll split the ship in two. By the time they realize you weren't fooling, help should arrive."

So the magician did as he was told, and put on a lively and entertaining show, pulling rabbits out of his hat and making things mysteriously disappear. Then he noticed the captain frantically signaling to him. Obediently, the magician announced: "Ladies and gentlemen, for my final illusion, I shall split this ship in two."

At that moment, the iceberg was reached. The ship rocked with the impact and listed dangerously to one side. The passengers fell into a state of panic. Half of them were thrown into the sea.

Amidst all the brouhaha Mr. Finkelstein, clinging to an upside-down railing, bumped into the magician. Shaking his head disapprovingly, Finkelstein snarled, "Wise guy!"

Remember Me Fondly

Sheila joined the girls for mah jongg one day sporting a huge diamond ring. All the ladies were envious. Finally, one of them asked where she'd gotten it.

"Well," said Sheila, "my mother-in-law gave me a thousand dollars in trust before she passed away. She said that when she dies, I should buy her a beautiful stone for her memory. So I did!"

A MOTHER TORE INTO her son's bedroom and shook her son who was lying in bed. "Mike," she said, "you've got to go to school. Enough of this nonsense, get up and go to school."

Mike growled, "I don't wanna go to school."

She shook him once again and said, "Mike, I'm telling you, you've gotta get up and go to school."

Mike said, "Why?"

"Well," she yelled, "I'll give you three good reasons. In the first place, I pay taxes; in the second place, you're 50 years old; and in the third place, you're the principal."

TWO PARTNERS IN THE GARMENT industry were having business problems; it looked as if they might have to declare bankruptcy. But at the brink, a particular line of dresses seemed to lure a buyer. A West Coast outlet wanted to buy the whole line, at a price which would put the partners well into the black. The partners were overjoyed.

"The only thing is," warned the buyer, "I have to have the deal approved by the home office. I'm sure they'll agree, but I do have to check with them. I'm going back tomorrow. If you don't hear from me by Friday closing time, you can be sure everything's okay."

The week went by slowly; and Friday crawled. The two men sat without moving at their desks, unable to concentrate on any kind of work. Without this deal, they would definitely go under. They sweated the hours out, minute by minute.

Two o'clock went by, three o'clock, then

four o'clock, and now they were close to pay dirt. Four-thirty came, and they were holding their breath. Suddenly, a messenger burst into the office. "Telegram!" he said. The men froze in terror.

Finally, one of the partners stood up. Slowly he opened the telegram, and read it quickly.

Then came a shriek of joy. "Harry! Good news! Your brother died!"

But You Didn't Ask Me That!

A young fellow was up for membership at a very exclusive club where Jewish people were not welcome. As his name was Baker, he thought they might not figure out his true identity.

The day of his interview with the membership committee, the young man took great pains to dress carefully and make an elegant appearance. One committee member asked, "Did your parents come from Russia?" His reply was a simple, "No."

Since they had no real grounds on which to base their suspicions, the board accepted Baker. But several weeks later, an investigator gave the committee the facts. Summoned before the committee again, Baker was asked, "Why did you lie to us? We asked you if your parents came from Russia and you said no."

"Well, they didn't," answered Baker. "They're still there!"

Mum's the Word

Golda and Becky got together for their usual morning cup of coffee.

"Did you meet that new woman who moved in across the street?" asked Golda.

"Did I ever!" exclaimed Becky. "She couldn't stop complaining about her husband."

"Believe me, there's nothing worse than a complaining wife," said Golda. "Now take me; my husband drinks too much, he gambles, he stays out late—a worse husband you never saw in your life. But do *I* ever say anything to anybody?"

THREE OLD JEWS were sitting around drinking tea and philosophizing about life. One said, "You know, it is my opinion that the best thing there is in life is good health. Without good health, life isn't worth a darn."

The second took exception. "Well," he said, "I've known plenty of rich men who were sick, terribly sick. But they had lots and lots of money and they went to the best specialists. They went through all kinds of treatments and operations and they came out almost as good as new. The fact is that without money life isn't worth much. You can be as robust as a lion and still be miserable if you don't have a red cent. On the other hand, with money you can buy practically anything. In my opinion, the best thing in life is to have money."

The third one had listened patiently. And now he demurred, saying, "Yes, health is good, and money is good, but I've seen people with plenty of money who are utterly miserable,and I've seen people in good health who were miserable. The fact is that rich or poor, healthy or sick, life in itself is an enormous overwhelming misery. In my opinion, the best thing in life really is not to be born at all."

The other two responded to this remark by plunging themselves into deep contemplation. Finally, one broke the silence. "Yes, Danny, you're right. The best thing in life, as you say, is not to be born at all. But, tell me, who can be so lucky, one out of a million?"

By Any Other Name

Mrs. Feldstein stopped in at the deli to get herself a nosh. "How much costs today a pickle?" asked Mrs. Feldstein.

"A pickle," replied the grocer, "is a nickel."

"A *nickel*?" Mrs. Feldstein looked around some more. She picked up one of the smaller pickles. "Well, how much is this *shtikl*?"

The grocer came over to where she stood. "That *shtikl* is a nickel," he answered.

"My God! . . . And this *pickeleh*?" pointing to a still smaller pickle.

"That *pickeleh* is a *nickeleh*!"

A CATHOLIC PROFESSOR once asked an orthodox rabbi to explain the meaning of the Yiddish word *farblundjet*.

"It means having wandered off course, to be lost, to have gone astray," replied the rabbi. "For example, when I began my rabbinical career, I was really *farblundjet* (confounded); I occupied a reform pulpit for two years."

"Is that so?" said the professor. "Were you unfrocked?"

"No," explained the rabbi, "just unsuited."

HARRY CAME EAST to visit cousin Ben in New York. Ben showed Harry the sights, and wound up the day by taking him for his first meal at the Automat.

Harry was delighted. He gazed at the display cubicles endlessly. His cousin, meanwhile, sat down to eat his meal. When he had finished and cousin Harry was still not in sight, Ben went to look for him. He found him at the apple pie slot, putting in nickel after nickel.

"Are you crazy?" exclaimed the cousin. "You already have fifteen pies!"

Harry chuckled gleefully and continued feeding coins into the machine. "So what does it bother you," he said, "if I keep winning?"

What Are Fathers For?

Mr. Shapiro was sitting in the living room with his son Mark. "Dad, what's the tallest mountain on earth?" the boy asked.

"I don't know," admitted Mr. Shapiro.

A few minutes passed, then Mark asked, "Dad, who was the king that came after Napoleon?"

Mr. Shapiro thought and thought, but finally he had to say, "I don't know."

Some more time passed and Mark spoke again. "Dad, why does the moon always have the same side toward us?"

"Oy," Mr. Shapiro heaved a huge sigh, "I don't know."

Then he looked at Mark's disappointed face and remembered what he had always been telling him about the importance of an education. He clapped his son on the shoulder and said cheerfully:

"Ask, Mark, *ask*! How else will you learn?"

A LEARNED MAN went into his library to read, but he couldn't find his glasses. He looked and looked, but couldn't locate the missing glasses. So he used the logic of his ancient people, reasoning thusly:

"Hypothesis: *Maybe* someone came in and stole my glasses while I was having lunch? *No!* Why not? Because *if* it was someone who needed glasses to read with, he would own his own; and if he *didn't* need glasses to read with, why would he steal mine?

"Second hypothesis: Maybe a *thief* stole my glasses, not to use but to sell! But to whom can you sell a pair of reading glasses? *If* the thief offers them to someone who needs glasses, *that* man surely owns a pair already; and *if* the thief offers them to someone who *doesn't* use glasses, why should such a man buy them? No!

"So, where does this take us? Clearly the glasses must have been taken by somebody who needs glasses and has glasses, but cannot find them. *Why* can't he find them? Perhaps he was so absorbed in his studies that, absent-mindedly, he pushed his glasses up from his nose to his forehead, then, forgetting he had done so—took mine!"

The answer began to dawn on the scholar. "I will push that reasoning even further!" he thought. "Perhaps *I* am that man—who needs glasses, owns glasses, and moved his glasses up to his forehead, and forgot that he had done so!"

"If my reasoning is correct, that's where my spectacles ought to be right now!" And with that he moved his hand up to his forehead, right on top of his glasses. So he smiled, pushed them down, and went on with his reading.

YETTA WAS WALKING up and down the block, waving hello to her neighbors, hoping one of them would notice her new dress.

Essie Mandelbaum did notice, and she called out to Yetta, "I like your dress!"

"Oh!" Yetta responded artfully. "This little *dresska*! It's nothing. I only use it for street-walking."

Total Transformation

A businessman was sitting quietly in a restaurant eating his lunch when suddenly a stranger hailed him.

"Hey there, Weinstein!" shouted the man. "My goodness, what happened to you? You used to be short, now you're tall. You used to be blond, and now you're dark-haired. You used to have blue eyes, and now they're brown!"

The businessman was polite but firm. "I beg your pardon, sir, but my name's not Weinstein."

"My God!" exclaimed the other. "You changed your name, too!"

The Lord Works in Strange Ways

There was a young reform rabbi whose hobby was golf. Having a large congregation, however, he didn't often have time to relax. He missed playing very badly.

So the rabbi searched his calendar and found that he had only one free day—and not another for the next six months! But that day was a Saturday. Could he dare slip off after services on this one day for his favorite sport? The rabbi decided quickly, mumbled an apology to God, and on Saturday drove off to a course thirty miles away to play unrecognized.

Up in heaven, an angel looked down, and to his horror, he noticed who was on the golf course. Immediately, God was notified and asked what should be done.

God was greatly saddened. He leaned out of heaven, and with a mighty force, blew a strong gust of wind straight down onto the golf course. The rabbi was on the second hole when the heavenly breeze caught up with him, and that gust took the ball from the tee just as the rabbi swung. Up went the ball, straight down the fairway to make a miraculous hole in one. The angel was aghast.

"But why did you do that, Lord? Is that what you call a punishment?"

The Holy One smiled. "Think about it," said God. "Who can he tell?"

A MATCHMAKER TOOK a well-to-do man to meet a prospective bride and her family. While they were waiting in the living room, the matchmaker pointed to the elegance of the surroundings.

"These people are well off. Look at this fine furniture. Take a look at the delicate dishware. Notice the paintings on the wall and the sculpture on the mantel."

The businessman was suspicious. "To make a good impression on me, perhaps they have borrowed these things."

At that, the matchmaker scoffed, "Borrowed? Don't be foolish! Who would lend anything to such paupers?"

THE TEACHER ASKED little Morris whether the world was round or flat.

Morris thought a moment, then said, "I guess it's neither, because my dad's always saying that it's crooked."

Summer Doldrums

The week after Labor Day, Abe Cohen and Nat Goldfarb met for lunch. They hadn't seen each other for several months. As they sat down, Abe began complaining.

"Nat, my friend, I have just lived through a summer the likes of which I never thought I would see. June was already a disaster. Never in my entire business career have I seen a June like that. Yet when July came I realized that June had been quite good, for with July I went down through the floor and into the sub-basement. July was absolutely unbelievable and indescribable, and when I tell you—"

But at this point Nat interrupted impatiently. "For heaven's sake, Abie, why are you coming to me with these piddling matters?" he said, even more depressed than his friend. "If you want a tale of *real* trouble, here it is. Yesterday my son, my only son, on whom I had been placing all my hopes, came to me and told me he was getting married to another boy. Do you hear me? My son has become an open homosexual! What can be worse than *that?*"

"I'll tell you," Nat answered, "August!"

A MATCHMAKER PROPOSED a beautiful young girl to a businessman client as a possible bride. The client was reluctant to pursue the matter because he didn't possess, in his opinion, enough money for such an attractive girl.

"Oh, you needn't worry about that," assured the matchmaker. "You'll never have to support any of her family; the girl is an orphan."

The meeting was arranged. Several weeks later, the man complained to the matchmaker. "You lied to me!" he said. "The girl is not an orphan. She not only has a father who's alive and well, but he is living in prison!"

The matchmaker shrugged. "You call that living?" she asked.

A RABBI AND A PRIEST were talking one day. They were longtime friends and knew each other well.

"Tell me," said the priest, "have you ever tasted ham? Be truthful now."

"Well," the rabbi became uncomfortable, "once, when I was in college. Curiosity became too much for me and I had a ham sandwich." The priest smiled benevolently.

"But now tell me," the rabbi went on, "and be truthful, did you ever, perhaps, make love to a girl—"

Then the priest began to stammer. "Well, once, when I was in college, *before* I was ordained . . ." he sputtered.

The pair were quiet for a moment. Then the rabbi smiled. "It's better than ham, isn't it?"

MOISHE AND BECKY went to City Hall to apply for a wedding license. They were directed to the third floor where they had to fill out forms. When that was done, they were to take the forms to the sixth floor, pay a fee, and then they'd get their license.

They obediently filled out the forms, went up to the sixth floor and waited on a line. Eventually, they came to the front of the line, where the man looked over the forms.

"Becky?" he said. "Your legal name isn't Becky, is it? Go back to the third floor and fill out a new form with your real name, Rebecca."

So the couple went back downstairs, filled out another form, returned to the sixth floor, waited on line, and arrived before the man again.

This time the man got up to the part with Moishe's name on it. He frowned, "Moishe? That doesn't sound like an English name to me."

"Well, my real name is Michael," said

Moishe, "but I've always been called Moishe—"

"Go back down to the third floor," interrupted the man, "and fill these forms out in English!"

So the couple went down again, filled out another form, came back up to the sixth floor, waited again on line, and eventually arrived at the window. The names were okay this time, but this time the man found the address unacceptable. They had written Williamsburg, New York. "Williamsburg is just a section of Brooklyn," said the man. "Go downstairs and rewrite the forms, and this time write 'Brooklyn, New York' instead of 'Williamsburg, New York.'"

Moishe and Becky went through the whole procedure yet another time and returned to the sixth floor. Finally, after several hours at City Hall, everything seemed in order.

Moishe sighed and turned to Becky. "It's worth it, sweetheart. Now our little boy will know that everything is legal."

The official glared at them. "Did I hear you say you have a little boy?" Moishe admitted they did.

"You already have a baby and you're just getting a wedding license today? Do you know that makes your little boy a technical bastard?"

Moishe was icy. "So?" he countered. "That's what the man on the third floor said *you* are, and *you* seem to be doing all right!"

Mrs. Rosen was at a hotel in the Catskills, sunning herself by the pool, when a group of ladies asked if she would like to join them in a game of mah jongg. Mrs. Rosen was delighted.

So the ladies began to play, apparently welcoming Mrs. Rosen into their circle. But suddenly, one of the women raised a hand to gain everyone's attention.

"I think we ought to inform Mrs. Rosen about our rules for conversation," she said. "Mrs. Rosen, there are some subjects we never discuss. We never discuss husbands: they are all miserable. We never discuss fur coats: they are all gorgeous. We never discuss grandchildren: they are all geniuses. And we never discuss sex. What was, was."

There's a Reason for It

An old Jewish story tells that at the time of creation, all creatures were told what their functions would be in the world, and each was asked how long he would like to live.

The horse was told that it would spend its life running around at the mercy of men who would ride on its back. Hearing this, the horse asked for a lifetime of only 20 years.

The donkey, next in line, was told that it was destined to carry heavy loads. Hearing this, the donkey said 20 years would be enough for him, too.

Next in line, so the tale goes, came a cantor. He was told he would spend his life singing, so he asked for 60 years.

The angels thought that 60 years was quite a lot, and they suggested to the cantor to shorten his request to 40 years. But the cantor insisted.

So the angels took ten years from the life of the horse, and ten from the life of the donkey, and added these years to the forty reserved for the cantor.

And that's why a cantor sings like an angel for the first 40 years of his life, then for the next ten he sounds like a horse, and finally during his last ten he brays like a donkey.

Jacking Up the Profits

Morris had just started his new job as a bus driver and he approached his work conscientiously. For five straight days, his fares totaled a steady $75. No matter how diligent he was, he always ended the day with the same $75.

The following Monday, however, Morris proudly handed the company cashier a pouch containing $314. The bus official was astonished. "Fantastic!" he said. "How did you do it?"

"It was easy," explained Morris. "After five days on that cockamamy route, I figured business would *never* improve. So I drove over to 14th Street, and worked there. I tell you, that street is a gold mine!"

Never As Bad As It Seems

A struggling farmer was burdened down with the support of a sick wife, seven children, and a mother-in-law, all in a one-room shack. Eventually, it grew too much for him, and he sought counsel from the rabbi.

"Do you have a goat?" asked the rabbi.

"Why, yes," answered the peasant.

"Take the goat into your home."

"But rabbi! There's no room as it is!"

"Just do as I say, and come back in a week."

So the farmer took the goat from the field, and brought it into the small house.

Next week, the peasant came again to the rabbi and said, "Rabbi, it's driving me wild."

"Do you have any chickens?" asked the rabbi.

"Yes, I have four—"

"Take them all into your home."

"But rabbi—"

"Just do as I tell you."

So the bewildered man took the chickens from their coop, and put them in his one-room home.

Next week, the farmer came to the rabbi and said, "Oh, rabbi! It's terrible! The goat's messing up the floor; the chickens are flying all over and messing everything up! We're going stark mad."

"Do you have a cow?" asked the rabbi.

"Yes," sighed the farmer.

"Bring the cow into the room," commanded the rabbi, "and come back next week."

The crestfallen man left in despair. That week he lived in hell. The cow mooed, the chickens cackled, and the goat bleated. The ever-present noise was awful. And the one-room had turned into a sty.

The following week, the man returned to the rabbi. He was thoroughly beaten. He poured out to the rabbi a pitiful tale of woe.

The rabbi listened patiently and then commanded, "Take all the animals out of the house, and put them back in the field. And come back tomorrow."

The man did as he was told. When he returned the following day, the rabbi asked, "Nu? How are things?"

The farmer replied, "Oh, rabbi, everything's wonderful. And so quiet! So roomy!"

A Tradition

Goldberg and Levine were sitting on the porch after supper.

"Did you hear about the accident Stein had in his new car?" asked Levine.

"How could I not?" answered Goldberg. "It was in front of my house, wasn't it? I've got eyes, haven't I?"

Levine continued, "Were you sitting right there when it happened?"

"What then?" answered Goldberg. "I was maybe lying here? Have I got a bed here?"

Levine was exasperated. "Goldberg, why do Jews answer a question with another question?"

Goldberg answered, "And why not?"

STEINMEIER HAD JUST run an extremely successful campaign to promote his company's product. In fact, sales had soared and he had earned so much money that he determined to take his first trip abroad.

His travel agents laid out an elaborate route which, among other things, brought him to Rome. In Rome, Steinmeier arranged for an audience with the Pope. Standing before the Pope, Steinmeier advised his Holiness that he had been a longtime admirer of the Catholic Church and was willing to make a donation of $5,000,000 to the papal treasury, provided, of course, that his Eminence would grant one very small request.

The Pope was extremely gratified. He had certain repairs of the Vatican in mind which $5,000,000 would make possible. If the request were not too difficult he most certainly would accede to it. What did Steinmeier want?

"Ah," said Steinmeier, "every day millions of Catholics say The Lord's Prayer. I would like," Steinmeier said, "a slight textual change ordained by you. Where it says, 'Give us this day our daily bread,'" Steinmeier explained, "would you be so kind as to issue a bull changing it to 'Give us this day our daily pumpernickel.'"

Don't Count on It

Israel has always encouraged immigration. But for a while it looked as if there wouldn't be enough money to care for newcomers as well as the already established Israelis. The financial situation was bad.

Several cabinet members met to discuss the situation. "I have an idea!" said one. "Why don't we declare war on the United States? They're bound to win, and you know how they treat their victims. They'll come into our vanquished country and build up our industry, give us money for roads, food for relief, and so on!"

"That's a wonderful idea," replied another minister. "But what if, with our hard luck, we win."

ONE VETERAN OF Miami Beach had been coming every winter for twenty years. One day, she spotted an old friend from New York on the beach.

"Sadie!" she called out. "It's so good to see you! How are you?"

"Molly!" cried the other. "Actually I'm not feeling so good. That's why I came down here for a week."

Molly thought for a minute, then she asked discreetly, "Darling, have you been through the menopause yet?"

Sadie looked at her. "The Menopause? I told you I just arrived. I haven't even been through the Fountainbleau yet!"

Universal Language

A tale is told of a certain countess who was half French and half English. When she was in labor with her first child, her husband was beside himself with anxiety. The doctor tried to calm him down.

"She's got plenty of time to go," he said. "Let's play cards."

So he dealt out a hand. But then suddenly a cry came from the bedroom above: *"Mon Dieu! Mon Dieu!"* The count jumped up from his chair.

"Not yet. Not yet," soothed the doctor. "Keep on playing." So they did.

But again came a wail: "Oh God. Oh *God!*" The husband was on his feet again. And still the doctor did not look up. "Not *yet*," he insisted. "Not yet. Your turn to play!"

A few minutes later, the voice upstairs cried, *"Oy ge-valt!"*

Then the doctor stood up and declared: *"Now."*

Deep Communication

Moishe and Izzy sat in the restaurant for several hours without uttering a word. They drank tall glasses of tea with lemon. As each finished his glass, he signaled the waiter to bring him a refill.

After a long while, Moishe finally broke the silence. "Oy vey!" he sighed.

Five minutes later, Izzy replied. "You're telling me!"

Nothing But the Best

Ginsburg was swimming at the beach when suddenly he got a cramp. He couldn't swim back to shore. So he started yelling, "Help! Help!" Then he was overcome with panic, and started to drown.

Luckily, rescuers got to him in time. Quickly they pulled him out of the water and onto the beach. "Give him artificial respiration!" someone shouted.

Suddenly, the man's eyes fluttered open. "No!" Ginsburg cried weakly. "Not artificial, please. Give me the real thing—I can afford it!"

GREENSTEIN AND HIS FAMILY decided to move from New York to the Pacific Northwest.

"But what will you do there?" asked his friends.

"I'm strong," said Greenstein. "I'll be a lumberjack."

So the family moved West. Greenstein went out to look for a job as a lumberjack. The first foremen he met was impressed with his muscles, but wanted a physical demonstration of strength. He pointed to a tree with a twelve-inch trunk and asked Greenstein to cut it down. Greenstein did it in one minute.

"I can't believe it," said the astonished foreman. "My best cutter couldn't do that tree in less than four minutes! Please, Mr. Greenstein, do

just one more so I know my eyes aren't deceiv-
ing me."

He pointed to a tree 16 inches thick. Greenstein downed it in two minutes.

"That's unbelievable, Mr. Greenstein. That
tree would have taken any of my men ten minutes! Tell me, where did you work before this?"

"Well," said Greenstein modestly, "when I
learned lumberjacking, I was in the Sahara."

"In the Sahara?" The foreman was in-
credulous. "But there are no trees in the Sahara!"

"Not any more there aren't."

Heart to Heart

Two old buddies, Sam and Irv, met by chance
one day.

"It's good to see you, Irv," said Sam. "So
how are you?"

Irv gave a shrug and replied, "Ehhhh. . . !"

Undaunted, Sam continued, "And how's
your wife?"

Irv shook his head from side to side, rolled
his eyes skyward, and said, "Eh-eh!"

"And how's business?" Sam persisted.

Irv moved his arms up and down with an
unsteady motion. "Mm-mmm," said he.

"Well, so long, Irv," said Sam, as he turned
to leave. "It's been nice to see you. You know,
there's nothing like a good heart-to-heart talk
between friends!"

COFFEE
36¢ A DOZEN

SAMMY FELL VICTIM to inflation and found he had to give up his business. After a while, he didn't even have money left for food, and was reduced to begging in the streets.

A businessman walked down the street, and Sammy decided he might be the generous sort. So he approached the man and said, "Sir, can you spare three cents for a cup of coffee?"

The man looked surprised. "Where can you get a cup of coffee for three cents?" he asked.

"What do you mean 'where?'" Sammy scoffed. "Who buys retail?"

Never Too Late

An eighty-year-old widower announced one day that he was taking a bride of twenty-three. Needless to say, his family was quite distressed; they tried every means to dissuade him. But nothing worked.

So they appealed to their rabbi, a young

man of rather liberal views. The rabbi promised to talk to the old man. But when he visited the prospective groom, he found his arguments were to no avail.

But the rabbi had a suggestion. Why not also take in a boarder? The rabbi reasoned that the old man would not be able to share his bride's youthful energy, and she would soon grow tired of his inertia. With a boarder, the young girl could still tend to her husband, while the young boarder would provide her with proper companionship.

It was a revolutionary concept, but it had merit. The old widower thought about it and agreed. "Sure, I get it," he said. "My family won't like it, but what business is it of theirs? If I am satisfied, why should they object? And the young lady, as you say, would be taken care of in the way of companionship, and so on."

The rabbi felt he'd done a good deed, and left for his summer vacation with a sense of accomplishment. When he returned, he went immediately to see how the newlyweds were doing.

"I want you to know we are both very happy," said the old man. "What's more, to the surprise of my family, my wife is pregnant."

"Oh," smiled the rabbi. "I suppose, then, you took in a young boarder as I suggested."

"Yes, I did," exclaimed the old man. "And she's pregnant, too."

Izzy WAS LOOKING for ways to improve business, so he decided to paint a new sign to hang over his door. Neatly he blocked out the letters: "FRESH FISH SOLD HERE DAILY."

Mendel came by and stood over Izzy's shoulder. Finally he couldn't resist saying, "I don't mean to butt in, Izzy, but that's a ridiculous sign."

"What do you mean?" asked Izzy.

"*Fresh* fish, Izzy? No one would ever dream you sold fish that weren't fresh—unless you call it to everyone's attention in a sign like that."

"You're right," said Izzy, and he put white paint over the word FRESH.

He started to lift the sign to hang it up, but Mendel broke in again, "Izzy, I hope you don't think I'm kibitzing too much, but SOLD? You don't need to say that; you certainly don't give the fish away for nothing."

"That's true," said Izzy, and he whitened out the word SOLD.

"And while you're at it . . . you don't need to say HERE. After all, you don't sell them *there* or anyplace else *but* here."

So Izzy painted out HERE.

"Okay now?" he asked.

"We-e-ll," said Mendel, "as long as you asked, I think you should take out DAILY too. After all, if the fish are fresh, they must come in daily."

"Of course," said Izzy, and he hung up the sign, which now read: FISH.

Mendel left and along came Irving. "Izzy, what are you doing with that crazy sign?" said Irving.

"It's to advertise my business," said Izzy.

"You don't need to advertise, Izzy," said Irving. "Your fish smell all the way down the block. Everyone can't help but know what you sell."

"Right!" said Izzy, and he took down the sign.

One-Upmanship

"My wife," said Koblinsky, "is so educated, so well read, that she can talk for hours and hours on any subject you name."

"Huh," scoffed Michaelson, "that's nothing. My wife can talk for hours and hours and doesn't even require a subject."

SAMUEL RABINOWITZ summoned his son. It was time, he thought, for the young boy to learn the facts of life. He took the lad into the parlor, closed the doors, and said, "Benny, you're old enough now. I'd like to discuss the facts of life with you."

"Okay, Pop," said Benny, "what do you want to know?"

Honesty Is the Best Policy

A farmer was on his way to town when he found a wallet in the road. Looking through the wallet he found $90, a name and address, and a paper stating: "If found, please return this wallet. $10 reward."

The farmer quickly changed routes and brought the wallet back to its owner. But instead of being grateful, the owner said, "I see you have already removed the ten dollars due you for your reward."

The poor man swore that he had not; the owner insisted that $10 was missing. "There was a hundred dollars in that wallet!"

So they took their tale to the rabbi, who listened patiently to the farmer, and then to the owner of the wallet. "Who will you believe, rabbi," ended the rich man, "that ignorant farmer or me?"

"You, of course," answered the rabbi. The farmer was aghast.

But then the rabbi took the wallet and handed it over to the farmer. Now it was the owner's turn to be astonished. "What are you doing?" he sputtered.

"You said your wallet contained one hundred dollars. This man says the wallet he found contained only ninety. Therefore, this wallet can't be yours," said the rabbi with finality.

"But what about my lost money?" cried the indignant man.

Patiently, the rabbi explained, "We must wait until someone finds a wallet with one hundred dollars in it."

It's Never Too Soon

A delighted grandmother was asked to babysit for an afternoon with her daughter's two little boys. The happy trio set off for the park and a picnic.

On the way, the woman ran into an old friend. "How are you?" she greeted her warmly.

"I'm very well, thank God," replied her friend. "And these must be your grandchildren. How old are they?"

The grandmother puffed with pride. "Oh! The lawyer," she said, pointing, "is two, and the doctor is going on four!"

He Couldn't Win

Sarah Finkel sat next to a handsome business-man on a flight to Miami, and finally could not resist asking, "Pardon me, sir, but are you Jewish?"

The man lifted his eyes from the newspaper in which he'd been buried and said, "No madam, as it happens, I am not."

Mrs. Finkel thought about it for awhile, and when he'd become engrossed again in his article, she asked, "Are you *sure* you're not Jewish?"

The man kept his temper and explained, "Madam, I have nothing against the Jews, and if I happened to be Jewish, I would be glad to admit it. It just happens that my ancestors are not Jewish. Please forgive me for that." Then he noisily lifted his paper and began to read once more.

Mrs. Finkel hesitated another few minutes. Then she said, "Listen, are you absolutely *positive* you're not Jewish?"

The businessman, seeking quiet, decided there was only one way to get it. "Well, Madam, you're right. I *am* Jewish."

Then Mrs. Finkel looked at him quizzically and said, "Funny, you don't *look* Jewish."

Bird Brain

Izzy's friend Yosef said he had found a parrot that not only would speak, but could speak

Hebrew. Izzy was skeptical, but when he went to Yosef's house, they put a yarmulke on the bird's head, and the parrot immediately recited the full Friday night services.

Izzy was amazed, and begged his friend to let him buy the bird. After much cajoling, Yosef agreed. For the price of ten dollars, Izzy was able to take away the *dovvining* bird.

On Rosh Hashonah, Izzy took his bird to the synagogue. He passed the word around that his parrot could sing the prayers. Everyone laughed at his pretensions, and he extracted wagers of 10 to 1 that his bird couldn't follow the service for even three minutes.

When the prayers began, Izzy put a yarmulke on the parrot's head and commanded him to sing. But the bird was silent.

"Go, pray, like you did for Yosef," Izzy urged. But the parrot wouldn't open its beak.

"Pray, you numbskull! I have a bet on you!" But the parrot wouldn't utter a sound. Finally, Izzy had to admit defeat, and left the synagogue downcast and deep in debt.

When he got home, he lashed into the bird. "So you shame me in front of everybody, eh? So you make me lose ten to one bets? So you pretend you don't know how to pray? Why did you do that?"

Finally, the parrot spoke up. "Don't be stupid!" said the parrot. "Comes Yom Kippur, you'll make a killing!"

MRS. MOSKOWITZ was aging. She had passed 81 and was having some "woman trouble." Upon the advice of her daughter, she went to visit a gynecologist. She remained quiet throughout the examination, but when it was over she turned to Dr. Lipsky.

"Dr. Lipsky," she said, "you seem to be such a nice young man. Tell me, does your mother know how you're making a living?"

MRS. ECKSTEIN DRESSED her little girl Barbara in her prettiest outfit and took her shopping in New York's fashionable stores.

When they finished, they walked to the subway on Lexington Avenue. As the pair crossed Fifth Avenue, suddenly little Barbara sneezed. "*Gesundheit*," said her mother in cultured tones.

They walked a little further, and as they got to Madison Avenue, Barbara sneezed again.

"God bless you, dear," intoned Mrs. Eckstein, still in a dainty voice.

But when they reached Park Avenue, Barbara sneezed yet again. And then again. At this, Mrs. Eckstein gave her daughter a good wallop. "With all my other troubles," she hollered, "you gotta go and catch a cold!"

You Gotta Be Firm

Steinberg had been having his lunch in the same Lower East Side restaurant for 20 years. Every day, he left his office at noon, went to the restaurant, and ordered a bowl of chicken soup. Never a change.

But one day Steinberg called the waiter back after receiving his soup.

"Yes, Mr. Steinberg?" inquired the waiter.

"Waiter, please taste this soup."

"What do you mean, taste the soup? For 20 years you've been eating the same chicken soup here every day, yes? Has it ever been any different?"

Steinberg ignored the waiter's comments. "Please, taste this soup," he repeated.

"Mr. Steinberg, what's the *matter* with you? *I* know what the chicken soup tastes like!"

"Taste the soup!" Steinberg demanded.

"All right, all right, I'll taste. Where's the spoon?"

"Aha!" cried Steinberg.

Maybe You Know Him?

Steinmetz and Rosencrantz were Jews living in Berlin during the early years of World War II. Steinmetz had proper papers; Rosencrantz did not.

They were walking down the street one day, when they saw an SS officer approaching. Rosencrantz thought quickly. Pointing to his left he said, "Steinmetz, you run in that direction. The Nazi will chase you, and then I'll be able to get away."

So Steinmetz tore off in the direction indicated. Sure enough, as soon as he saw Steinmetz bolt, the SS man pursued hot on his trail, allowing Rosencrantz to quietly disappear. Several blocks later, when Steinmetz could run no farther, he stopped to catch his breath, his heart racing madly.

When the SS officer caught up, he was in a rage. He demanded to see Steinmetz's papers. Steinmetz produced the documents; the policeman examined them minutely but found that all were in order. "So why did you run, eh?" he asked.

"Well," answered Steinmetz, "my doctor told me I must run at least a mile after each meal."

"Uh, huh," said the Nazi skeptically. "But you saw me racing after you. Why didn't you stop then?"

"Well," answered Steinmetz, "I thought maybe you go to the same doctor!"

Shocker

An old man faithfully bought a lottery ticket every week.

Well, it happened that the week came when he held a winning ticket. When his wife read the number in the paper, she was overcome with joy.

But suddenly, she was afraid. How should she tell him about it! He had a weak heart, and the shock might kill him. So she asked a friend of her husband's, who was very good at that kind of thing, to break the news to him.

The friend did a splendid job of drawing out the tale. By the time the news was out the old man had had plenty of time to get used to the idea of winning.

"It's great news, indeed," said the winner. "But why did you take such a roundabout way to tell me?"

"We were afraid that with your heart, it might come as too much of a shock."

"You are a kind man and a good man. And now, I'll tell you something. I'm going to give half the money I won to you. How do you like that?"

The usually loquacious friend didn't say a word. He had had a heart attack!

Forever Is a Long Time

Moishe slipped in front of a department store. In the freak accident, he broke both his legs. After several months, all the bones healed. His family now persuaded him to sue the store for damages on the grounds that he'd been permanently crippled.

So Moishe got himself a wheelchair and a lawyer and he sued. And despite testimony from the insurance company's doctors, Moishe's pitiable appearance won him the sympathy of the court. He was awarded $30,000.

When the insurance man came to deliver the check, he was shaking with fury. "We know you aren't permanently crippled," he stated. "And, so help me, we're going to follow you all the days of your life until you stand up and walk out of that wheelchair. And when you do, we'll take your picture and sue you for all this money and more!"

But Moishe maintained he was permanently crippled. The man handed him the check, and then begrudgingly asked what Moishe would do with it.

"Well, me and my wife, we've always wanted to travel," said Moishe. "So we're going to fly to Scandinavia, and then on through Switzerland, Italy, Greece—and I don't care what agents and spies with cameras are following me because I'm going in my wheelchair. And then, of course, we'll go to Israel; then to Persia and

India, and across to Japan and the Philippines—and I'm still going to be in this wheelchair. So I don't care about your people who are following. And from there we are going all across Australia, and then to South America, and then all the way up to Mexico and through the western U.S.A. and cross-country to Canada and across again to France."

He paused for breath, and then went on. "And there, we're going to visit a place called Lourdes. And there, you're going to see a miracle!"

Togetherness

Mrs. Meyerowitz met Mrs. Goldstein for a cup of tea one afternoon.

"Did you hear that the Martinsons' stove exploded last night?" began Mrs. Meyerowitz. "Mr. and Mrs. Martinson were blown right out the front door and into the street!"

"If that's true," quipped Mrs. Goldstein, "that's the first time they've gone out together in thirty years."

HARRY HAD HEARD OF a tailor who was supposed to be a genius. A business associate who recommended him certainly wore good-looking suits. So Harry went downtown to see the man.

"Sure, I can make a suit for you, mister. But it'll take me thirty days."

"Thirty days!" cried Harry in dismay. "Why, it only took God six days to make the entire universe!"

"*Nu*," shrugged the tailor, "and look at what he turned out."

SAM BROMBERG HAD BEEN a cutter for some 20-odd years. All his life he had dreamed of owning a Cadillac.

But when Sam got to the point where he had actually saved up enough money to buy such a sumptuous car, he suddenly collapsed at his table and died.

His friends conferred about his burial. One of them spoke up and said, "You know, all his life Sam dreamed about owning a Cadillac. I think it would be fitting and proper if we took the money that he saved up and purchased the best Cadillac on the market and buried him in it." The other friends agreed.

On the day of the funeral, all Sam's friends gathered around the burial plot, which was about ten times as large as an ordinary grave. Six workmen had been employed to dig the grave. While the service was being intoned, the huge

Cadillac was lowered from a crane into the grave.

One of the workmen lifted his head and marvelled at this brand new shining monster of a car coming down into the grave. In the front seat sat Sam all dressed up in white coat and tails. The workman nudged the man next to him and exclaimed, "Oh boy! That's the way to live!"

Rewriting History

Young Samuel arrived home after his first day at Hebrew school.

"Well," said his mother, "tell me what you learned today."

"Today we learned about Moses," answered Samuel.

"And what do you know about Moses?"

"Well, he was this general, see. And he got all the Jews together in formation and marched them out of Egypt, with General Pharaoh's Egyptians hot on their trail. And then in front of him, there was the Red Sea blocking his path. So Moses ordered bombs dropped, and bang! The waters parted just long enough for the Jews to get across. And when the Egyptians followed, they were all drowned."

The mother was aghast. "Is that how they teach the story of Moses nowadays?"

"No, Mom," answered Sammy. "But if I told you the story the way the teacher told it to us, you'd never believe it."

The Heart of the Matter

Moe met Sammy for a glass of tea.

"So how's business?" asked Sammy.

"Fine," said Moe, "except for one thing."

"And what is that?"

"It's rotten."

IN A LITTLE TOWN in Russia, there were many more girls than boys. Consequently, the local matchmaker was having an easy time making good matches for the young men of the village, although the girls were often ending up with the poor end of the bargain.

A rather unpleasant man in the village, whose face matched his disposition, wanted a bride who possessed beauty, charm, and talent.

"I have just the girl for you," said the matchmaker. "Her father is rich, and she is beautiful, well-educated, charming. There is only one problem."

"And what is that?" asked the young man, suspiciously.

"She has an affliction. Once a year, this beautiful girl goes crazy. Not permanently, you understand. It's just for one day, and she does not cause any trouble. Then afterwards, she's as charming as ever for another year."

The young suitor considered. "That's not so bad," he decided. "If she's as rich and beautiful as you say, let's go to see her."

"Oh, not now," cautioned the matchmaker. "You'll have to wait to ask her to marry you."

"Wait for what?" pursued the greedy man.

"Wait for the day she goes crazy!" came back the answer.

For the Price, It's Worth It

Moe went to a department store to buy himself a suit. He found just the style he wanted, so he took the jacket off the hanger and tried it on.

A salesman came up to him. "Yes, sir. It looks wonderful on you."

"It may *look* wonderful," said Moe irritably, "but it fits terrible. The shoulders pinch."

The salesman didn't bat an eye. "Put on the pants," he suggested. "They'll be so tight, you'll forget all about the shoulders!"

JAKE WAS FURIOUS. He had just gotten an anonymous phone call telling him that his partner Sam had been fooling around with his wife. Jake couldn't wait until Sam got into the office; he ran out to Seventh Avenue looking for him. Between 37th and 38th Streets, he found him.

Rushing up to him, Jake yelled, "You no good bum, you untrustworthy bastard. Here you're supposed to be my friend and I find out now that you've been fooling around for months with my wife Becky. I got a good mind . . ."

At this point Jake grabbed Sam by the lapel. He stopped his tirade and exclaimed, "Oh, what a nice piece of goods!"

WELL-TO-DO FINANCIER Otto H. Kahn was being driven through New York one day when he passed a storefront sign reading: "Abram Cahn. Cousin of Otto H. Kahn."

The banker was furious at the misrepresentation and had his lawyer call the store immediately and threaten proceedings if the sign was not removed.

A few days later, Kahn asked his chauffeur to drive him past the store again, to see if the man had kept his promise. Sure enough, the old sign was gone. In its place was a new sign, which read: "Abram Cahn. *Formerly* cousin of Otto H. Kahn."

If at First You Don't Succeed

Max had been living with his shrewish wife for thirty years. But he couldn't stand the nagging any longer. He consulted his friend Shmuel about what to do.

"Why not do her in?" suggested Shmuel.

"If I do that I'll be thrown in jail. I don't want to spend the rest of my life in prison."

Shmuel considered, then he said, "Well, why don't you buy her a car? She can't drive. Maybe she'll have an accident, and her death won't be on your head."

So Max bought his wife a little sportscar. But when he met Shmuel a week later, he still looked sad. "She drives it perfectly," said Max. "I threw my money away."

Shmuel knew what was wrong. "That car you bought her was too small. Why don't you get her a large car that will be hard to handle? She's bound to get into an accident with a big sedan."

So Max bought his wife a huge Cadillac. But that didn't work either. "She drives that one perfectly, too," he told Shmuel a week later. "What do I do now?"

"Well, there's one other thing you can try. Splurge and get her a Jaguar."

So Max bought his wife a Jaguar. A week later, he was all smiles.

"So what happened?" Shmuel asked him.

"Wonderful!" exclaimed Max. "One bite, and she was finished!"

As Simple as That

Mrs. Diamond had wheedled some money from her husband to have the house redecorated, and she hired an interior designer to help do the job.

"All right," said the decorator, "now how would you like it done? Modern?"

"Me, modern? No." said Mrs. Diamond.

"How's about French?" asked the decorator.

"*French?* Where would I come to have a French house?"

"Perhaps Italian provincial?"

"God forbid!"

"Well, madam, what period *do* you want?"

"What period? I want my friends to walk in, take one look, and drop dead! Period!"

IT WAS BERNIE'S first day as a health-insurance salesman. For his first prospect, he was given the name of the president of a big corporation. If the man bought a policy, Bernie was empowered to speed up proceedings by bringing back a urine sample for processing the same day.

Bernie was gone all morning. When he came back that afternoon, he was carrying the signed policy and a large bucket.

Pleased with himself, Bernie showed his boss the policy. "That's great," the boss smiled. "But what's in the bucket?"

"What do you mean 'what's in the bucket?'" Bernie puffed with pride, "I sold the company a group policy!"

Being Specific

Two men sat down in a restaurant and ordered their main dishes. Then they closed their menus. The waiter said, "Thank you, gentlemen. And would any of you wish a beverage with your meal?"

One man said, "Well, I usually have coffee, but today I think I'll have a glass of milk."

The other man said, "That sounds good. I'll have milk, too. But make sure the glass is clean!"

"Very good," said the waiter, and he left.

Soon he came back with a tray and two glasses of milk, and said, "Here you are, gentlemen. Now which one asked for the clean glass?"

Code

The premier of Russia didn't like the adverse publicity his country was receiving about its treatment of Jews. So he had the most prominent rabbi in the country brought in.

"I want you to write a letter to the prime minister of Israel, telling him how wonderful it is for Jews to live in this country. And I want to see it before it gets sent."

The rabbi said nothing but he gave it a great deal of thought and then sat down to compose his letter. He wrote of what a paradise it was in Russia and stated that a Jew couldn't find a better place to live. Then he added: "However, there are shortages; there are no candles and no sugar."

The premier was pleased with the letter until he read the ending. "What do you mean by this?" he cried. The rabbi explained that if he didn't somehow qualify the glowing praise, the letter wouldn't sound realistic, and the Israelis would think it had been forced from him.

"Quite right," the Russian official agreed. "Send it off."

When the Israeli cabinet was shown the letter, they were somewhat puzzled. But the prime minister, who knew Yiddish, had no trouble deciphering the message.

"Obviously, the letter is for propaganda purposes," he said. "And the message in the ending is quite easy to understand if you think about it. He's talking to us in Yiddish. He says there are no candles—that means it's dark. He says there is no sugar—that means it's not sweet. If it's not sweet, it's bitter. He's saying, *es is finster und bitter* (it's dark and bitter). That means things can hardly be worse."

To CELEBRATE LITTLE HOWIE'S bar mitzvah, Mr. and Mrs. Shapiro sought something unique. The usual catered affairs were a thing of the past. All year long, Howie's friends have been having miniature-golf bar mitzvahs, amusement-park bar mitzvahs, and Broadway-show bar mitzvahs. For weeks, the Shapiros racked their brains trying to come up with something that hadn't been done before.

Finally Mr. Shapiro decided. "We'll have a safari bar mitzvah! Hang the expense! We'll charter a plane for all our friends and relatives and fly to the depths of the jungle."

All the arrangements were made. Soon the great day came. Led by a native African guide, the bar mitzvah party made its way along the safari trail.

They had only been hiking a few minutes when the guide came to an abrupt halt. Impatiently, Mr. Shapiro asked, "What's happened? Why are we stopping?"

The guide replied, "We'll have to wait here for awhile. There's another bar mitzvah right ahead of us."

Finding a Way

Izzy had spent his whole vacation in Spain without seeing a bullfight. On the last day, his tourist guide said to the group, "I hope you have all seen at least one bullfight. A trip to Spain would be incomplete without witnessing our national sport."

That afternoon, Izzy went to the bull ring, but all the tickets had been sold. So he walked morosely around the outside of the bull ring, wondering what to do.

Suddenly, a man passed in front of him, walked up to a small door, and knocked. A voice from within called, "Si?"

The man answered, "Toreador!"

The door opened to admit him.

Curious, Izzy waited. Sure enough, another man came along, knocked on the door, shouted, "Matador," and was admitted.

Boldly, Izzy walked up to the same door and knocked. The guard called, "Si?"

In response, Izzy shouted, "Isador!"

The door swung open and the guard greeted him with open arms, *"Kumpt arayn!"* (Yiddish for "Come in!")

A BOASTFUL WOMAN, sitting on the sands of Miami Beach, informed her companions, "Last year I went to Europe three times."

One of the women answered, "So what's so special about that? I came from there."

A MERCHANT MOVED DOWN SOUTH from New York into one of the backwater towns. He seemed to be doing rather well, but then at about the beginning of April, the sales started to slacken very noticeably.

Sam Cohen pondered and pondered about the cause of the decline in business. Suddenly he realized, as he walked the streets, that every other establishment on Main Street had an Easter sign out front and that all the windows were especially dressed for the holiday.

Sam was in a quandary. He was a religious Jew—how could he, in good conscience, pay obeisance to Easter? He was up all night thinking. The next morning he arose and his face was beaming. He had worked out the solution.

That afternoon, Cohen's general store also contained an Easter sign. It read: "Christ is risen, but Cohen's prices are still the same."

Self-Reliance

In 1948, when Israel declared its independence, Velvil Pasternak flew at once from New York City to offer his services to the fledgling state. He applied at the recruiting office to join the beleaguered Israeli Army.

After the usual forms were completed, he was told to go down to Section 1 and pick up his Army gear. He came to the first window and the clerk asked him what size shoes he needed.

"Size 8-1/2," answered Velvil.

The clerk looked around in the stockroom, came back and said, "I'm sorry, we don't have 8-1/2. We're very short of shoes. We got size 8 and we got size 9, but no 8-1/2's."

Velvil hesitated, but the clerk advised, "Look, what do you need shoes for? You got sneakers on. It's perfectly okay. Better than to have shoes that are too small or too big. Forget about shoes. Wear your own sneakers."

Velvil agreed and went to the next window, where he requested a medium-size army shirt. The clerk looked around and came back. "Look, we got size small army shirt and size extra large. Medium we ain't got." Then he looked at Velvil and said, "Look, that shirt that you've got on. That's pretty good. What do you need an army shirt for? Use what you've got."

Velvil agreed and moved on. He went through this at each commissary window and came out with his original set of clothes.

He was then ushered into the medical office. The doctor examined him and asked a few standard questions. "Do you swim?" he asked.

"What?" exclaimed Velvil. "Ships you ain't got neither?"

JACK SILVERS wanted to entertain his mother, so he bought two front-row-center seats and accompanied her to the Barnum & Bailey Circus. His mother watched all the acts disdainfully. Nothing seemed to please her. She wasn't at all impressed by the lion tamer; the dancing elephants didn't amuse her; the tumblers left her cold. Then the main act was announced. Hidalgo would walk a tightrope fifty feet in the air while playing a violin.

Jack nudged his mother and said, "Ma, watch this. This is the big one. Don't be frightened. This is gonna be great!"

His mother didn't change her expression. To the applause of the crowd, the man walked across the tightrope playing one of Mozart's minuets in a manner worthy of a concert hall. Then, to everybody's amazement, he took one foot off the tightrope, and standing on tip-toe he played Beethoven's Moonlight Sonata.

Jack Silvers crowed, "Well, Ma, what do you say to that?"

"Well," conceded his mother, "okay . . . but a Heifetz he ain't."

Plain Logic

The poor tailor was beside himself. His wife was sick and perhaps dying. He called on the only doctor nearby.

"Please, save my wife, doctor! I'll pay anything!"

"But what if I can't cure her?" asked the doctor.

"I'll pay whether you cure her or kill her, if only you'll come right away!"

So the doctor promptly visited the woman, but within a week, she died. Soon a bill arrived charging the tailor a tremendous fee. The tailor couldn't hope to pay, so he asked the doctor to appear with him before the local rabbi to arbitrate the case.

"He agreed to pay me for treating his wife," stated the physician, "whether I cured her or killed her."

The rabbi was thoughtful. "Well, did you cure her?" he asked.

"No," admitted the doctor.

"And did you kill her?"

"I certainly did not!" expostulated the physician.

"In that case," the rabbi said with finality, "you have no grounds on which to base a fee."

Foreign Intrigue

The Russian Intelligence Agency intercepted a message that showed that Israel had just made an important atomic discovery. Anxious to find out what the Israelis were up to, a Russian agent was dispatched immediately.

The mission was top secret. The agent chosen was a very trusted and experienced man. He was given a name to contact in Tel Aviv, a guy by the name of Weinstein. The password was "Volga boatman."

The agent flew to Tel Aviv one evening. Early next day he went to look up the contact. To his dismay, when he arrived at the apartment house, he found that three different Weinsteins were listed as living there.

There was nothing to do but try them all one at a time, hopefully hitting the right one the first time. The agent knocked on the door at the first floor. "Yes?" said a man.

"Is your name Weinstein?" asked the agent.

"Why, yes," replied the Israeli.

"Volga boatman," said the Russian.

"Oh," grinned the man. "You want Weinstein the spy. He lives two flights up."

THE SCENE takes place in Tsarist Russia.

Shmuel Ginsburg was walking across a bridge over the Dnieper River. Through some accident he slipped and fell off, landing in the icy cold waters below. Through chattering teeth he screamed for help, and in a moment or so two policemen rushed to the rail of the bridge. But when they peered down into the waters and saw by his beard and by his dress that he was a Jew, they shrugged their shoulders, laughed with amusement, and were about to take off.

Ginsburg knew that he couldn't survive the cold. Desperate situations give rise to desperate remedies, and Shmuel was suddenly seized with an inspiration. With his last bit of strength, he yelled to the departing policemen, "Down with the Tsar." At once the policemen turned back. Here was sedition in full cry. They jumped into the water and dragged Ginsburg out to escort him handcuffed to the police station.

Catechism

Mr. and Mrs. Solomon had been trying for weeks to find a decent apartment. Finally, in Washington Gardens, they located an apartment that was just perfect. But their elation was followed by dismay when they realized that the renting agent was not disposed to lease an apartment to people of the Jewish faith.

Jake Solomon would not give up so easily.

Confronting the renting agent, he said, "You don't want to rent me an apartment because you think I'm Jewish, but you're wrong. I'm Catholic."

"Catholic?" echoed the renting agent incredulously.

"Yes, I'm a practicing Catholic. Just ask me any question you want and I'll prove it."

The renting agent snorted, "Huh, with a name like Jacob Solomon, I just don't believe you can be Catholic."

"Well," persisted Jake, "just go ahead. Ask me! Ask me!"

"Okay," the renting agent said, "what are the three members of the Holy Trinity?"

Jake grinned and said, "Why that's A-B-C, that's for kids. God, the father; Jesus, the son; and the Holy Ghost."

"Right," admitted the renting agent, "but, as you said, that was just A-B-C. Let's go on. Who was Mary married to on earth?"

"Oh," said Solomon, "every Catholic knows that the husband of Mary was Joseph, the carpenter."

"Right again," admitted the renting agent, "but now tell me this. Why was Jesus born in a stable?"

Solomon didn't hesitate a moment. He shot right back. "That's easy, too. Because bastards like you wouldn't rent apartments to Jews like us."

An Unusual Stance

Bernie was coming down the street when he noticed his friend Moishe coming toward him. But Moishe was walking funny. He had his elbow stuck out on his left side with the hand resting on the hip. Bernie stopped him:

"Moishe, what's with you? I know you and respect you for twenty-five years already, and suddenly you start to walk down the street in this fancy stance. What's going on?"

Moishe looked down at his arm and clutched his forehead in consternation. "Oh, my God! Gussie will kill me! I lost the pumpernickel!"

Don't Look at Me!

A professor was about to set out on an expedition to Africa and the Near East and he needed an assistant. So he put an advertisement in the newspaper requesting a man who spoke foreign languages, loved to travel, was able to use a gun, and so forth through a long list of qualifications. It was a pretty rare man who could fit his demanding specifications, and there were no responses to the advertisement.

But at the end of a week, one fellow did appear. He was short, unmuscular, unimpressive, but the professor interviewed him anyway.

"Do you like to travel?" asked the professor.

"Me?" said the man. "I hate traveling. Boats make me seasick, planes I wouldn't get on, and trains are the worst of all."

"But you are a linguist," continued the professor, "I presume you speak Urdu, Arabic, Turkish—"

"Who, me?" interrupted the little man. "I know nothing but Yiddish."

"Well, can you use a gun?" the professor persisted.

"Me? I'm afraid of firearms."

"Well," the exasperated professor exploded, "then what did you come here for?"

"I saw your ad. And I just came to tell you that on me you shouldn't rely."

Willing Spirit, Weak Flesh

A study group had been meeting for years, to study the Talmud. One member of the group had a pernicious habit of sipping a little brandy during the meeting. One night he drank just a little more than usual and became quite tipsy.

His companions decided to teach him a lesson. While he was in his drunken stupor, they carried him off to the cemetery and laid him prone among the tombstones.

After awhile, the Talmudic student woke up. He looked about him frightened and aghast. Then he started to reason, "Am I alive? Or am I dead? If I'm alive, what could I be doing here in the graveyard on top of the graves? And if I'm dead, then why do I feel that I must go to the bathroom immediately?"

A WIDOW FOUND HERSELF in dire financial straits. She decided to go and bake bagels, but after two months she found that her coffers were still quite empty.

In desperation, she repaired to the cemetery with the idea of consulting her husband who was lying there under the sod.

The *shamas* (beadle) of the town knew of the woman's proclivity in that direction. He placed himself behind the tombstone of the late departed.

The woman fell upon the grave and sobbed, pouring out her heart to her dead husband. "Oh, Isaac, Isaac, I don't know what to do. I can't get along without you. Oh, Isaac, I baked bagels but from that I cannot make a living."

There emerged a voice from the back of the tombstone, "So don't bake."

The woman called out in desperation, "But Isaac, oh my Isaac, if I don't bake bagels from where will I make a living?"

And the *shamas'* voice responded, "So bake."

IT WAS A FEARFUL NIGHT. Lightning shot through the sky and the thunder roared in blasts that would frighten anybody. The rain came down in sheets.

The door of a little bakery opened and a drenched man came up to the counter and said, "Let me have two bagels."

The baker looked at him incredulously. "What," said the baker, "you came out on a night like this just for two bagels? That's all?"

"Yes, that's all," answered the man. "That's all I need. Just one for me and one for Pauline."

"Who's Pauline?" asked the baker.

"Oh what the hell difference is it to you?" answered the man. "Pauline is my wife. Who do you think she is? Would my mother send me out on a night like this?"

Sign Language

There is a tale told that in the Dark Ages, the Pope suddenly decided he didn't want the Jews living in Rome anymore; they were all to be banished. The Jews grew afraid, for outside of Rome lay the darkness of rural medieval Europe. They begged to be allowed to stay.

The Pope listened to their pleas and agreed to give them just one chance. But he set forth a very strange condition. He would permit a debate—all in pantomime—pitting a nuncio against any Jew. If the Jew should win, his people could stay in Rome. Otherwise, out they would go.

But what kind of a possibility was this the Jews wondered. The Pope himself was to be the judge of the debate and the losing debater would be executed. How could anyone win against such a set-up! No one in the Jewish community could possibly accept the role.

But the sweeper of the synagogue volunteered. He would debate. Everyone knew the sweeper was surely going to his death. But what could they do! There was no way to save him from death and the Jewish community from exile. There was not even any way that the Jewish scholars could prepare the sweeper for the debate.

The day of the debate came. Everybody sat in the arena in complete silence.

The nuncio began by raising one finger and moving it across the sky. The sweeper instantly gestured firmly at the ground. The Pope looked uneasy.

Then the nuncio lifted one finger again, and this time pointed it squarely at the sweeper's face. The sweeper quickly pointed three fingers at the nuncio with complete assurance. And now the Pope really looked uncomfortable.

The nuncio now reached deep into his pocket and withdrew an apple, which he showed to the Pope. At this, the sweeper took out a paper bag from his pocket, and withdrew a piece of matzoh.

The Pope now announced that the debate was over. The sweeper had won; the Jews could stay in Rome.

"Your Holiness!" cried the churchmen

when the crowd had dispersed, "Why did you award the Jew the verdict?"

"That man," answered the Pope, "was a master of debate. When my nuncio swept his hand across the heavens to indicate that God ruled over everything, the Jew gestured toward the ground, indicating that the Devil also held sway of a world all his own!

"When my nuncio lifted one finger to indicate that there was only one God, the Jew instantly lifted three fingers to indicate the three aspects of God, the Holy Trinity.

"When my nuncio took out an apple to indicate the error of science that teaches the earth is round as an apple, the Jew countered by producing a flat piece of matzoh, to show that the Bible teaches the earth is flat."

The Jews, overjoyed, toasted and feasted their beadle. Then they begged him to explain how he had bested the nuncio.

"What's there to say?" he answered. "First, the priest waved his hand like he's saying 'The Jews must get out of Rome.' So I pointed downward to say 'Oh yeah! The Jews are going to stay right here!'

"Next, he points a finger at me as if to say 'Drop dead! The Jews are leaving.' So I point three fingers at him to say, 'You drop dead three times. The Jews are staying.'"

"And then?" asked the amazed congregation.

"And then I saw he was taking out his lunch, so I took out mine!"

Modern Art

Jake Mazeltov was walking along Fifth Avenue when he bumped into an old friend whom he had not seen for 20 years. "Joe Pasternak! My God, you haven't changed a bit! Am I glad to see you! Tell me, what're you doing?"

"Well," smiled Joe, "I'm an artist. As a matter of fact, I've done very well. I've got a picture hanging in the Modern Museum, right here off Fifth Avenue."

"You don't say!" exclaimed Jake. "Gee, that's marvelous. Say, we're not far from there. Could you take me over and show the picture to me?"

"With pleasure," said Joe, and they strolled over to the Modern Museum.

There on the wall, Joe pointed to his picture. It was brown all over, almost a solid monochrome, with only a deep patch of darker brown in the lower right-hand corner. Jake looked at it quizzically for a few minutes but got nothing out of it. He turned to his old pal Joe and said, "What is this picture supposed to represent?"

"Well," said Joe, "it's modern art. The name of the picture is 'A Cow in a Field.'"

"'A Cow in a Field!' My god, Joe, what d'ya mean, a cow in a field? I don't see any field there. A field is green. Where's the green?"

Joe explained patiently, "Well, see in modern art it doesn't go quite that way. The cow walked into the field and he ate up the grass, so now the grass is all gone; there's no more green, there's only brown."

"Okay," said Jake. "So where's the cow?"

"Well, the cow, he ate up the grass already, so of course he just went on, that's all."

"Oh," said Jake, "now I understand. There's no green because there's no grass; there's no cow because the cow went away." He said, "But there's a big patch of brown in the right-hand corner, now what's that?"

"Oh, well, you've gotta understand, this is modern art," said Joe. "A cow eats up a whole field of green grass and he walks on, but on the way out what d'ya think he does?"

Almost Perfect

A matchmaker was exulting over the virtues of a particular girl. "She is beautiful, tall, well-built, a good cook, a smart woman, with integrity," she listed.

But the client said, "But you left out one important thing, didn't you?"

"Not possible!" said the matchmaker. "What could I have left out?"

"That she limps!" said the young man.

"Oh!" came the answer, "But only when she walks!"

MRS. MELTZER INVITED her new neighbor in for a cup of coffee, and to show her around the house.

"What a beautiful lamp!" admired the neighbor.

"Yes," said Mrs. Meltzer modestly, "I got it with Bleach-o detergent coupons."

"And I like that painting on the wall!" the neighbor went on.

"I got that with Bleach-o coupons, too."

"Oh, a piano! I've always wanted a piano."

"Well, as a matter of fact, I got that piano from Bleach-o coupons, too."

Then the neighbor tried one door handle that wouldn't budge. "What's in that room?" she asked full of curiosity.

"Bleach-o detergent! What else?"

We Can Always Find Room

Mr. Likovsky was a meat wholesaler in New York for forty-five years, and when he retired he was rich. But he didn't care so much for the money; his dream was to move to Israel.

So he sold his belongings and boarded a ship for a new life in a new country. He was so glad to be in Israel that he sent his entire savings in a check for two million dollars to the prime minister. The prime minister was extremely grateful. If there was anything he could ever do for Mr. Likovsky, a phone call would be all that was needed.

Well, as a matter of fact, there *was* something he could do. Mr. Likovsky had always wanted to be in politics. Was there some position in the Israeli government he could have?

The prime minister thought long and hard. After all, Mr. Likovsky had had no formal training in government, and his background wasn't suitable. He would consult his ministers.

At first, the ministers were outraged. But with a little thought, they found just the spot. The gave Mr. Likovsky a position with the Ministry of Health and Welfare. His job was to be at the pier every time a ship left Israel. He would stand with a megaphone, announcing to departing visitors: "*Foor Gezunta-hite!*" (Yiddish for "Have a healthy pleasant trip!")

ONE DAY, FRIEDA TOOK her elderly grandmother to the museum. Everything went fine until they reached the collection of medieval religious art. Frieda hesitated, for this was a subject that she knew was far beyond her old grandmother and she anticipated difficulty.

They stood before a rendition of the nativity scene. Her grandmother stared at it curiously. She said, "Frieda, darling, I see the woman just had a baby, but there are animals around. Why would there by animals around a new-born baby?"

"Oh," answered Frieda, "the baby was born in a stable."

"Poor thing," answered her grandmother, "and she doesn't have any shoes and stockings on?"

"No," conceded Frieda.

"And a doctor I suppose she didn't have either?"

"No, Grandma, she was a very poor woman."

"But," responded her grandmother, "if she's so poor, how did she take it into her head to have pictures taken?"

WHY DOES A JEWISH WIFE close her eyes when having sex?

Heaven forbid she should see her husband having a good time.

Small Talk

Nate and Becky were spending a Sunday at the amusement park. They were having a lovely time. Then Nate decided to buy tickets for the tunnel of love.

The ride was slow and pleasant. When they emerged into the light, Becky smoothed down her dress, dabbed on her lipstick, and smiled shyly at Nate. She said demurely, "Nate, you know, you shouldn't have did it."

Nate turned to her and insisted: "I *didn't* did it."

Becky was flabbergasted. "What! *You* didn't did it? Well then, who *did* did it?"

Sorry I Asked

Feinberg was on the subway when a man came up to him and asked if he had the time. Feinberg didn't answer him. The man thought he hadn't heard so he asked again. And still Feinberg said nothing. Finally the man walked away toward the other end of the platform.

After he was gone, another rider approached Feinberg. "Excuse me, sir, but that seemed like a perfectly reasonable question. I notice you are wearing a watch. Why didn't you give him the time?"

"Well," replied Feinberg, "I'll tell you. I'm standing here minding my own business, and this guy wants to know what time it is. So maybe I tell him what time it is. Then what? We get to talking, and this guy says, 'How about a drink?' So we have a drink. Then we have some more drinks. So after a while I say, 'How about coming up to my house for a bite to eat?' So we go up to my house, and we're eating sandwiches in the kitchen when my daughter comes in, and my daughter's a very good-looking girl. So she falls for this guy, and he falls for her. Then they get married."

The other man was staring at Feinberg in utter amazement. But Feinberg went on.

"And any guy that can't afford a watch, I don't want for a son-in-law!"

Fishy Story

A ship came into port carrying a cargo of various products from Portugal. One part of the cargo remained unclaimed and the captain, in order to retrieve the shipping expenses, offered the bill of lading for sale. The cargo in question was a shipment of sardines.

A merchant coming aboard to claim his own cargo saw the unclaimed sardine shipment and negotiated with the captain. He wound up buying the sardines at 3¢ a can.

He paid for the shipment, took the bill of lading, and then, as he was leaving the ship, he met another merchant. He offered him the cargo of sardines at 5¢ a can. The merchant promptly accepted.

He in turn took the bill of lading down to the market-place and sold the shipment at 10¢ a can. The new buyer immediately sold it again at 15¢ a can.

Ultimately, the shipment was sold to still another merchant at 18¢ a can. This man, armed with the bill of lading, and all its endorsements, came down to the wharf to claim the cargo. The captain turned over the crate of sardines to him upon presentation of the bill of lading. The owner proceeded to open up one of the cans and stuff a sardine in his mouth. He promptly spewed it out again. "Yuck—ugh—uch! These stink! They're terrible!"

Witnessing his distress, the captain turned to him and said, "Don't you know? These sardines ain't for eating. They're just for buying and selling."

AFTER MANY YEARS of not having seen each other, Deborah ran into Rhea at—of all places—a bar mitzvah reception her boyfriend had invited her to.

The women shed tears, and immediately fell into deep conversation. Suddenly, the bar mitzvah boy walked in, to the applause of the assembled guests.

"Look at that poor boy!" Deborah whispered. "His face is so full of pimples, you could almost throw up looking at him!"

Rhea was scandalized. "It so happens," she announced haughtily, "that that's my boy, David!"

Deborah's face turned bright red, then she asserted effusively, "You know, darling, on him they're becoming."

FOR HIS BIRTHDAY, Mrs. Finkelstein gave her grown-up son Charlie two Dior ties. One was red and the other blue.

On his next visit to his mother, Charlie put on the red tie and strode into the apartment.

His mother took one look at him and sighed, "Ah! The blue one you didn't like."

A Wise Child

Little Bernie was seated with his tutor, studying the Holy Scripture. They came to the portion where the Good Book recounts that Dinah, the daughter of Jacob, had been sexually assaulted by the sons of Schechen. Bernie asked for clarification.

The rabbi said, "Well, let's take a look at the words of the great commentator Rashi."

The text said, "*And they lay with her and they afflicted her.*"

"Yes," said Bernie, "but what does that mean?"

Answered the rabbi, "Well, the commentator said '*And they lay with her*'—that means, in the ordinary manner; '*and they afflicted her*'—that means, in an extraordinary manner."

"Yes," said Bernie, "and what does 'extraordinary manner' mean?"

Whereupon the rabbi gave Bernie an enormous whack across the mouth and said, "And the ordinary manner you already know about?"

National Characteristics

Jake Weiss worked for a travel agency in Manhattan where he met people of all nationalities. Once, a friend asked him if he saw any differences among peoples of different countries. Did each nation really have a personality?

"Oh, definitely yes," said Jake. "When you tell an Englishman a joke, he laughs three times. Once when you tell it, to be polite. Then again when you explain it, also to be polite. Eventually, he'll laugh a third time—in the middle of the night when he wakes up from a sound sleep, and suddenly understands the point of the story.

"Now, when you tell a German the same joke, he'll laugh twice. First, when you tell it, in order to be polite. Then a second time when you explain it, also to be polite. There will be no third time, because he'll *never* get the point.

"If you tell an American the same joke, he will laugh once—immediately—when you tell it, because he'll get it right away."

"That's very interesting," said the friend. But Jake continued.

"And when you tell a Jew the same joke, he won't laugh at all. Instead, he'll say, 'It's an old joke; and besides, you told it all wrong.'"

EVERYONE ACKNOWLEDGED that the Jacobys were the happiest family in the neighborhood. They never quarreled about anything and always seemed to get along. One day, at a cocktail party, the neighbors and friends gathered around Jacoby and asked him how he could account for the marvelous success of his marriage.

"Oh," he said proudly, "Sadie and I made an agreement when we got married. She would make all the small decisions and I would make all the big decisions. And we've kept to that policy through all the years of our marriage."

"Like what kind of big and small decisions?" asked the curious audience.

"Well," explained Jacoby, "she makes the small decisions like who my son Milton is going to marry; who my daughter Jeanette should go out with; where we should go on our summer vacation; and how much we should spend, for example, on a bar mitzvah present for Tom Seltzer's son; how much we should pay for the maid. That kind of thing, you know."

"And the big decisions?" pursued the crowd.

"Oh," said Jacoby modestly, "I make the fundamental decisions. I decide whether the United States should resume relations with China. I decide how much money Congress should approve for Israel. And I decide who would be the best candidate for president."

A MAN CAME INTO a grocery store and asked for five cents worth of salt. The proprietor asked, "What kind of salt do you want?"

"What kind of salt do I want? I want salt, plain and simple. How many kinds of salt are there!"

"Ha ha," chuckled the store owner, "what you don't know about salt! You come with me." And he took him downstairs and showed him a cellar that contained no less than 40 or 50 barrels of salt. The customer was amazed. "All these are different salts?" he asked.

"Yes, they're all different. We have salt for all kinds of prices and uses."

"My goodness, you're a specialist. I suppose, if you have all these barrels of different kinds of salt, you must sell one hell of a lot of salt. You must really know how to sell salt!"

"Oh," said the other, "me—I'm not so good at selling salt, but the guy who sold it all to me, boy! Can *he* sell salt!"

Gentleman Caller

Sidney Blustone answered the doorbell. Opposite him, as he opened the door, he was startled to see a ferocious looking individual—hair disheveled, eyes bloodshot, hands nervously clutching and unclutching. The man announced, "I'm the Boston Strangler."

Sidney stepped back and shouted behind him, "Becky, it's for you."

A HART BOOK